THE

WEDDING CAKE

BOOK

WITH A SOCIAL HISTORY OF WEDDINGS

BY JULIE JONES AND GLENDA TRIGG

BELRIDE BOOKS

ACKNOWLEDGEMENTS

With the opening of our Celebration Cakes showroom in Melbourne, in July 1986, we realised a long-held ambition to display Cake Decorating to perfection in a retail environment.

With two exceptions, each of the beautiful cakes in this book has been commercially supplied to a bride's order. Whilst all do not necessarily comply with competition rules for cake decorating, they provide a unique insight into the diverse technical and creative abilities of one decorator supported by a small, but wonderful team of people.

To Glenda Trigg, I can only express the sheer joy of working with a professional whose performance under pressure has to be seen to be believed, and whose creative ability has been a total inspiration; to Margaret Mott for the patience to perform to a consistently high standard of covering day after day; to Shirley Herbert, Joyce Mitchell, Sue Oteri, Nancy Johnson and Patricia Brandi for the superb sugar flowers that tell a story all of their own; to Robyn Buckley and Franz Lohm in the bakehouse for the fruit cakes that begin each order; to Peter Mash and Ray Goodwin for their safe delivery each weekend; to James Flaagan for the translation of beautiful cakes into an exquisite photographic statement; to David Doyle–David Hughes Design Pty. Ltd. for the vision and understanding that brought this book to reality; to Lynette Kelly for her comprehensive research of the wedding ceremony and its fascinating traditions; to Tombi Peck for her interest and support; to Howard Cook and staff for the endless supply of cake boards; to Giselle Boothman for the lace panel; and finally to all the brides whose wedding cakes were the basis for this book.

Happy reading and happy decorating!

Julie Jones

To Tony and Nicholas

First Published by Belride Books 1988
Correspondence–71 Burwood Rd. Hawthorn 3122, Australia.

By Julie Jones and Glenda Trigg
Cake photography–James Flaagan A.I.P.P. Peter Foeden & Associates
Research and editing–Lynette Kelly
Design and production–David Doyle–David Hughes Design Pty. Ltd.
Proudly printed in Australia by Owen King Printers Australia Pty. Ltd.
Colour Separations by Image Scan Pty. Ltd.

ISBN-0-9587971-0-2
©Belride Books 1988

CONTENTS

INTRODUCTION

I was delighted to be asked to write the introduction to this beautiful book on weddings.

Although I am probably best known internationally as a cake decorating teacher, judge and author, I have also in my role as editor of a cake decorating magazine researched a great deal of the history of cake decorating, its folklore and traditions. I found this element of the book most stimulating. Also included in the following pages are many other traditions, superstitions and historical facts to do with the wedding itself. I am sure this will all be of great interest to any prospective bride.

The illustrations in the book are particularly beautiful and many brides will be inspired by them as they plan for their great day. It will also provide a new source of stimulation for the many cake decorators both new and experienced who are always on the lookout for any fresh ideas. Cake decorators throughout the world will be thrilled to know that a follow-on volume is planned to detail the making of the cakes, flowers and decorations featured in this book.

All too often a wedding cake has to be chosen in a situation that is not ideal; in a busy bakery, cake decorating supply shop or in a cake decorator's home quite possibly surrounded by their family! The elegant boutique run by Celebration Cakes must make this important facet of the wedding planning so much more pleasant for both the bride and her mother. The attractive surroundings featuring decorated cakes and delicate sugar flower sprays must provide the correct ambience and make the time spent on this task more enjoyable, if not easier, because of the many choices on display.

This book was written for the benefit of those of you not able to visit the boutique due to sheer distance, and provides a microcosm of what is available to the fortunate few who live in Melbourne and its surrounding districts. It will also serve as a marvellous memento to those of you lucky enough to have your special cake created by such talented, dedicated artists.

Tombi Peck.

Tombi Peck
Founding member of the
British Sugar Craft Guild

Glenda Trigg

THE GALLERY CAKE

The wedding cake has played a significant part at wedding feasts throughout the centuries. During the nineteenth century the bride cake became an important centrepiece of one or more tiers mounted on a silver stand.

The wedding cake–as it was now called–was a stately and magnificent castle of snowy white sugar with towers, festoons, leaves, doves, cupids and love knots, surmounted with a vase of flowers and trailing garlands.

It was important for the exhibition "Hatches, Matches and Dispatches," staged at the National Gallery of Victoria from the 24th November 1987 to the 31st January 1988, to display a Victorian wedding cake. This elegant cake was shown in the section of enchanting wedding gowns of the era.

Celebration Cakes was approached to make a replica cake and, with great enthusiasm, the staff spent several months researching English and Australian Victorian decorated wedding cakes. Finally a style was chosen, created in Australia in 1879.

The completed cake displayed the ornately piped patterns of the era, and was finished with waxed orange blossoms, sugar lilies, fabric flowers, feathers and pearls.

Rowena Clark

Rowena Clark.
Curator of Costumes and Textiles.
National Gallery of Victoria.

THE CAKE

oday, wedding customs world wide are remarkable for their similarity. In countries as diverse as China and Australia, England and Fiji, many of the same wedding traditions are found. Usually, they spring from the same sentiment–to bring the bride good luck on the day and in the future.

Three wedding traditions especially stand out because of their almost universal practice: adornment of the bride in a white gown, sealing the marriage with a ring or rings for the bride and groom, and the ceremonial cutting and eating of a special wedding cake.

ONE OF THE WORLD'S OLDEST TRADITIONS

The baking of a wedding cake is believed to be one of the oldest traditions in modern culture. It is not known exactly when the custom began, but by the time of the ancient Greeks and Romans, five thousand-odd years ago, it had become a well established part of every wedding celebration.

Today, when a bride and groom close their eyes to make a wish before cutting the first slice of their wedding cake, few pause to consider that this custom has been passed down from the Greek and Roman empires, to the Crusaders, the Saxons and the Norman conquerors, through Medieval England, the Restoration and the Victorian era and on to us in the twentieth century.

THE POWERFUL GOD OF THE HEARTH FIRE

When the Romans conquered Greece in 146 BC, they assimilated many Greek customs into their lifestyle and began to worship similar gods. The Romans continued to feed these gods on rich fruits, nuts and honey cake.

According to Roman custom, gods such as Janus, Venus, Jupiter, Juno, Mars and Vesta symbolised the powers of nature; while many hundreds of lesser gods were represented in everyday objects and in many events in a person's life. Within any Roman home there dwelt a god, or goddess, of the door, of the table, of the mat and so on.

These gods controlled all things, including family harmony. When a man decided to take a bride, his first consideration was not whether his parents would be happy, but rather whether his household gods would approve and be inclined to bestow their blessings upon the marriage. If a god was to take a dislike to a bride there would be no peace or happiness within their home.

Two household gods in particular had to be appeased following the celebration of a wedding.

The first was Vesta, goddess of the threshold, because she was the first immortal with whom the couple came into contact. Vesta was not a powerful goddess and bore little influence among the other gods of the house, so it was an easy matter to win her favour. The groom would simply carry his bride across the goddess's domain as a gesture of respect. (Vesta was also the goddess of virgins and it was considered highly disrespectful for a maiden about to lose her virtue to cross the domain of one who held virginity in such high regard.)

The second god, who dwelt in the hearth fire, was the most powerful within any home and he was not easily placated. Only the bride could appease the god of the hearth fire. To do this, as soon as she arrived home she would mix a wedding cake and offer it to the fire. After the offering had been made and the cake was baked, the bride was free to eat a little and so she became accepted as a member of the household. As other gods tended to follow the example of the god of the hearth fire, after this symbolic offering the bride and groom generally had no further trouble.

CAKE PACIFIED THE GREEK GODS

Greek gods were imagined to be common guests at weddings in 3000 BC. And each one was believed to have an enormous appetite which had to be satisfied if the marriage was to be happy and successful. Amongst the gods' favourite foods were dried fruits, nuts and small sweet honey cakes.

As the bride and groom left the temple after the wedding heading for their new home, friends of the newly-weds would pour bundles of these foods from their upper-storey windows in the hope that the gods would stop to eat and so be kept occupied, giving the bridal party and their guests time to enjoy the celebrations.

CROWNING THE BRIDE WITH CAKE

As the Roman civilisation advanced, their wedding ceremony became known by the name *confarreatio* due to the important role cake played in the ceremony.

During a marriage by confarreatio, a cake was baked of *far* and *mola selsa* by vestal virgins and then carried before the bride when she was conducted to the home of her husband. Outside the home, a sheep was sacrificed to the gods and the skin spread over two chairs for the bride and groom to sit upon. The marriage vows were then said in front of the pontifex maximus (head priest) and ten witnesses, and another sacrifice made. But the ceremony was not complete until the cake had been crumbled over the bride's head so that she would be blessed with an abundance of everything, especially children.

CAESAR BROUGHT THE CUSTOM TO ENGLAND

After Julius Caesar conquered Great Britain in 54 BC, many Roman wedding traditions became the custom in England.

Guests at a wedding for the son or daughter of a wealthy family copied the practice of breaking cake, or sometimes dry biscuit, upon the head of the bride. Poorer families scattered whole grains of wheat or corn in the hope that the marriage would be fertile.

Weddings in those days attracted quite a following. Often whole villages would turn out to join in the bridal procession as the couple made their way to their new home. The main attraction was the crumbs of cake or grain which tumbled to the ground, rather than the sight of a pretty bride. Uninvited spectators considered the leftovers quite a feast.

CAKE-CROWNING REMAINED FOR 2000 YEARS

As recently as 200 years ago, the best man and the first bridesmaid broke a biscuit or oatcake over the head of some English and Scottish brides as they crossed the threshold of the festive house after the wedding ceremony. By then, the tradition in England was about 2000 years old.

At a Scottish wedding, after the ceremony was concluded and the bride and groom were preparing to head to their new home, pipes would be struck up and the pipers would lead the company in a jig to the nearest inn for a celebration. As the bride entered the inn it was the privilege of the bridesmen to salute her by breaking an oatcake above her head, after which they would distribute the pieces, along with a glass of whisky, to everyone attending. An additional glass of whisky would be drunk at every inn passed along the way until the couple's new home was reached. There the celebrations were concluded by the drinking of a toast to the health of the bride, another to the bridegroom and a final drink to their clans.

WITH INCREASED WEALTH CAME RICHER CAKES

People began to substitute small rectangular buns–richly made from sugar, eggs, milk, spices and currants–for the oatcakes and biscuits as England became an increasingly wealthy country. The buns were made by the bride, her family and by many of the guests invited to the feast, resulting in a great quantity at any wedding.

Some of the buns were thrown over the bride's head as she arrived at the wedding banquet. Some were squeezed through her wedding ring and the pieces poured over her head, eaten by guests, or kept to be placed that night under the pillows of unmarried girls, who believed the cake would cause them to dream of their future husbands. Others were thrown to the poor folk who thronged outside the banquet house hoping to join in the celebrations. The remainder were built into a huge pile and set before the newly married couple. The bride and groom were expected to kiss over the piled cakes so that they would be blessed with many children and lifelong prosperity.

Once the small buns, each covered with sticky almond-paste, had been neatly stacked on a plate, it did not require much ingenuity to convert the pile into a single mass. With the production of these cake-piles, England had taken the first steps towards the concept of our *modern* wedding cake. But it was a good twenty years before the idea of baking and decorating one large cake for everyone to share caught on. And then it was a Frenchman rather than an Englishman who came up with the idea!

THE FRENCH FIRST ICED A WEDDING CAKE

When King Charles II was exiled in France and Oliver Cromwell was ruling England, the king and his courtiers developed a taste for French cooking and pastry, which they brought back with them after reclaiming the Throne in 1660. They also brought back some of the king's favourite French chefs to set up cookery schools throughout the country. These chefs and their students are now credited with having put the first touches to the slowly perfected modern wedding cake design.

The French chefs, who even then loved preparing food as much for its look as for its taste, found the piles of almond-paste buns at wedding feasts unattractive and unappetising. To compensate for the disorderly look of the pile and to make it more desirable they suggested it be iced with a crust of hardened white sugar and then adorned with trinkets and toys–tiny dolls, pots and pans, brooms, a bed–all indicative of the delights of matrimony.

The tradition of breaking the wedding cake over the bride's head lived on, even after it had become common practice to add the covering of sugar icing. In fact, with the addition of the sugar icing, the custom of crowning the bride with cake became much simpler. The sugary outer crust easily tumbled over the bride's head and shoulders while the cake itself remained intact for eating.

As time wore on, the bride's family began to provide two cakes as part of the wedding banquet. One was to satisfy sticklers for the old tradition, while the other, which slowly became more elaborate and highly decorated, was for those guests who had developed a taste for the sugar icing.

The two wedding cake tradition remained in many parts of the British Commonwealth well into this century. By that time one cake had become known as the bride's cake and the other was considered to belong to the groom.

When the custom of crowning the bride disappeared just before the reign of Queen Victoria, it was replaced by the much tidier procedure of cutting the groom's cake, always a dark fruit-cake, into small pieces and placing them in napkins or boxes for the guests to take home to enjoy later as a memento of the wedding. The bride's cake, a lighter mixture but more highly decorated, would be cut and eaten as dessert after the meal.

WEDDING CAKE IN OTHER CULTURES

Cake also played an important role in the ancient wedding ceremonies of many countries which never came into contact with the Greek or Roman empires. Brides in Asia, India, the Pacific Islands and Africa once all sealed their weddings by baking and eating a special cake. In these cultures, cake was considered representative of fertility. It was the end result of a plentiful harvest.

CHINESE BUNS

During preparations for an ancient Chinese wedding, when the bride was seated in a sedan ready to depart for her future home, her parents and other members of her family would take a bed quilt by its four corners and hold it before the bridal chair. One of the bride's assistants would toss four bread cakes into the air, one by one, so that they fell onto the quilt. The cakes had been sent earlier, along with many other wedding presents, from the bridegroom's family. The bride would repeat many quotations about the virtues of married life while the cakes were tossed. Then a large band would begin to play music, fire crackers would explode and finally the bride would depart from her father's home to that of her husband.

THROWING AWAY THE CAKE

In the African republic of Liberia, which was established by emancipated and escaped slaves from the United States of America, the custom of throwing a wedding cake over the roof of the groom's house was considered very important if a marriage was to be successful.

Before the wedding feast was over, the wedding party and all the guests would gather outside the bridegroom's house and the bride would throw a cake called *kolarh* as high and far as she could. It was believed that the higher the cake was thrown the happier the marriage would be. If it actually cleared the roof altogether the couple would enjoy a perfect life together. As the cake was made of a heavy dough and baked until it was hard and all the houses in the republic had very low roofs, brides rarely failed to ensure a lucky omen.

A CAKE FOUR DAYS IN THE MAKING

Once, in Macedonia, the four days leading up to every wedding were completely taken up with the preparation and baking of the wedding cake. If a wedding was to be held on a Friday, the bride and her friends would spend the preceding Monday and Tuesday sifting the grain to be used in the cake before taking it to the mill. On the Wednesday they could bring the milled grain home and together knead it into dough.

The kneading was done in a trough, over which a young boy with a sword and a small girl stood guard. The two children represented the husband, whose duty was to defend his household, and the wife, whose duty was to look after the home. The small girl had the additional duty of dropping a wedding ring into the cake dough when no one was looking.

On the morning of the Thursday the cake was baked and that afternoon part of it was broken over the head of the bride and groom, while the rest was eaten together with figs and fruit–symbols of fruitfulness and plenty. Whoever received the slice of cake containing the ring was said to be the next in line to marry.

On the Friday, after the wedding, a second cake in the shape of a ring was produced. The guests were allowed to eat half of this cake but the other half was kept by the best man for the bride and groom's breakfast the following day.

FIJIAN CAKE SYMBOLISED UNITY

It was once customary for a bride in the Fijian Islands to prepare a cake and some drink after her wedding, which she would begin to eat while sitting on her husband's knee. The groom would then finish the meal and the couple would crook together their little fingers, presumably as a symbol of their unity.

American Indians and some hill tribes of India also had customs similar to this involving the preparation and eating of a wedding cake.

Brides are traditionally expected to be at least a little late for their wedding. Even the groom can be excused for running a bit behind time. But there is no excuse for a best man who drags his feet.

Billie and Roy Gubbins were both at the church on time when they married at the Presbyterian Church Randwick, Sydney, on 5 January 1929. But their best man was nowhere to be found.

"When he did eventually show up, half an hour late, his excuse was that he had been busy playing A-grade cricket and try as he might he just could not get himself run-out," Billie Gubbins says, pretending to hold a grudge.

"Mind you, he was a pretty good cricketer," Roy adds. "He had started batting the day before the wedding. No one had any idea he would still be at the wicket the next day while we were waiting at the church. There wasn't much he could do about it except keep going while the runs were coming up."

The Gubbins wedding was, according to the two most important people there, typical of Sydney weddings in the 1920s. Billie wore a French lace wedding dress in a design similar to that worn by Queen Elizabeth, the Queen Mother. Following the fashion of the day, the dress had a dropped waistline and curved hemline, cut knee-length at the front draping down to a full length skirt and train at the back. The bodice was tight fitting with a scooped neckline.

Three generations of Billie's family were represented in the bridal party. "When Great-Aunt Lisa arrived from Scotland just for the occasion, we asked her to be the Matron of Honour," Billie recalls. "The other attendant was my sister. And my young brother was our page boy. He must have been about six or seven at the time."

"In those days, weddings were very big family affairs," Billie says. "Just about everyone in both our families was involved in the planning. My sister made my dress. She actually designed it herself. In fact, she was one of the best wedding dress designers in Sydney then. Her name was Margaret Small, till she married a Robertson."

"Weddings were also rather dressed-up affairs," Roy recalls. "I wore a black dinner suit and bow-tie and all the male guests were also in dinner suits. Except Billie's father. He wore grey striped trousers and a black, swallow-tail jacket. The ladies were all in smart cocktail frocks."

The 5th of January was one of only a very few days Roy and Billie Gubbins had shared together in the three years leading up to their wedding. "Our engagement lasted for three years, but I don't think we would have spent more than six weeks together in that whole time," Billie says.

"We met in Sydney, but just after our engagement was announced the company I worked for, Paramount Pictures, decided to transfer me to Adelaide." Roy adds. "There was no money around in those days for trips back home." "So we just had to keep in touch by writing letters," Billie interjects to finish off the story.

Billie and Roy are not sure if distance really makes the heart grow fonder, but the distance which had separated them certainly added to the enjoyment of their wedding day.

"The reception was good fun," Roy says as his mind travelled back to the Randwick Town Hall on a warm summer evening fifty-eight years ago. "There was a three-course dinner. I don't recall what we ate." "Oh, it would have been soup, then probably chicken, I think," Billie puts in. "Then we danced to a six piece band. And at the end of the night we cut a two tiered, round wedding cake, decorated with tiny white flowers and a plastic bride and groom."

Then, when it was all over, the happy couple hopped in their car and spent a short honeymoon travelling back to Adelaide–this time together.

DECORATION

ugar novelties were first used as decoration on cakes in England around 1660. Soon after this the idea began to spread throughout Europe. English, French and Italian pastry chefs all began a slow process of experimentation to determine how sugar icing could be improved, ornaments could be moulded and attached, and colours incorporated to create bigger and better examples of culinary art.

By the end of the seventeenth century, it was said that the fine arts numbered five: sculpture, painting, poetry, music and architecture. It was also said the cake decorator was the only artist who ever managed to master four of these five arts. The ability to play music was the only skill for which confectioners had no use.

As experiments proceeded, it became apparent that the only limitation placed upon a talented cake decorator was the capacity of his own imagination. People learnt to use their hands skilfully to mould shapes and icing bags were developed to facilitate piping. Accomplished decorators began to find design ideas in everyday things around them, from delicate lace patterns to imposing multi-storeyed buildings.

Soon, each country began to develop its own unique style of decoration, along with its own icing and cake recipes. But it is the British style, always executed upon a heavy, rich fruit cake, which has had the greatest influence upon wedding cake design.

THE ENGLISH STYLE

Originally, cake decorating in England was practised only by professional pastry chefs, who were quick to develop skills and perfect ideas. Competition was enormous, even as long ago as the sixteenth century. Every chef wanted to decorate a cake worthy of the king's table and so be accepted into court circles.

To stay ahead of other cake decorators, artisans were forced to attempt grand designs. Some chefs were known to invest a year in creating a masterpiece like the French Cathedral of Notre Dame in sugar. Even today, an insistence upon perfection of execution is a characteristic which distinguishes top English cake decorators.

English wedding cake designs fall into two distinct styles. One is known as the *Nirvana* style, the other features extensive over-piping work.

Under the school of Nirvana, cakes are covered completely or almost completely by 'run-on'

work. The end result has a fine porcelain-like finish. Cakes decorated in this fashion usually resemble an imposing building, sculpture or monument.

The architectural effect is achieved by drawing outlines of building structures–bricks, windows, doors and ornaments–and then flooding some outlines with detail. Windows may show picturesque garden scenes or beds of piped flowers, scenes in the couple's lives or anything else which strikes the decorator's imagination. The top of the cake is then finished off with a novelty bride and groom, wedding bells, horse-shoe or other ornament. A beautiful example of this style was Queen Elizabeth II's wedding cake (described on page 166).

The Nirvana style was one of the earliest established by English pastry chefs. From it came the idea to add over-piping, as chefs began to look for greater challenges and became more adventurous in their decorating techniques.

Cakes decorated with over-piping feature graceful curves and scrolls, especially around borders. All piped work is delicately proportioned and subtly coloured. The effect of different lines piped one on top of the other creates a strong three-dimensional effect. The result is a beautifully sculptured look, with the elegant often repeated curves providing continuity. It did not take long for over-piping to become a cake decorating style in its own right.

Piped or moulded flowers often feature in both Nirvana and over-piped cake decorating styles. In many cases however, the over-piping is so intricate, or the run-on work so descriptive, flower sprays take a second place in the overall look of the design.

AUSTRALIAN CAKE DECORATING

When Australia was settled cake decorating had been practised in England for more than one hundred years. By the time ladies in this new country found the time and could spare the commodities to produce their own culinary artwork another fifty years had gone by.

Cake decorating in Australia is newer than it is in any other country and, because of our early settlers' unique experiences, it has developed its own distinct characteristics.

Dainty is the term which best describes Australian cake decorating. Cakes and flowers are both kept small and flowers often appear isolated. Both Australian and English cake decorators prefer to hand mould each individual flower petal, gradually building the pieces to create a natural bud, rather than relying upon a standard cut-out shape. Every ornamental piece is produced in strict proportion to its real-life model.

Flowers adorning Australian wedding cakes are most often displayed in a discrete and airy way, rather than in masses or heavy clusters. This is possibly a reflection of the vastness of our great country and the amount of space early Australians found around them.

Two characteristics which have been developed to perfection by Australian cake decorators are extension work, where the icing is built out beyond the border of the cake, and feminine free-hand embroidery, produced by detailed execution using small piping tubes. Close-knit

embroidered lace patterns are often made off the cake and added to it as trimming.

Lace designs are sometimes piped onto fine tulle and then attached to cake tops and edges. Using this method, incredibly fine lines can be produced. The end result is an impression of still-life. Bows, butterflies, leaves and other delicate ornaments have been done in this manner to create unique effects.

SOUTH AFRICAN LACEWORK

As in Australia, cake decorating techniques originally borrowed from the English have been put to unique effect in South Africa. And again, as in Australia, lacework has become a characteristic feature of South African design.

South African lacework is usually extensive and showy. Especially popular are large lace wings, which dominate the tops of cakes and give the impression the whole arrangement could take off in flight at any moment.

The English Nirvana style is used extensively by the South Africans, who like to produce their run-on work in a strong three-dimensional fashion to create a dramatic overall picture.

Fruits, modelled in gum paste or marzipan and decorated in rich strong colours, are often featured on South African wedding cakes, as are flowers.

MEXICO AND THE PHILIPPINES

Two other countries are world-renowned for their individual cake decorating styles–Mexico and the Philippine Islands.

Beautiful clusters of flowers are found everywhere in the Philippines, including on wedding cakes. The more the better. Most flowers are moulded or piped on twisted wire to allow them to stand in dramatic fashion atop the cake.

Dramatic effect on a wedding cake in Mexico is created through stage-like settings. Gum paste dolls are meticulously moulded, dressed in detailed costumes and placed in realistic room settings or formal gardens. The Mexicans like their wedding cakes to tell the whole story of the courtship and marriage.

Two of the most noteworthy wedding cakes recorded in history are a Polish and an Italian creation.

The Polish cake was produced two hundred years ago for a very wealthy family. It has been described as a four-foot high edifice of sugar, representing the Temple of Hymen (which was built for the worship of Hymen, the Greek god of marriage). The temple was adorned with figures acting out a narrative. The whole effect was surmounted by the arms of the two families being allied by marriage.

The Italian cake was much simpler in its execution, although no less dramatic in its effect. About one hundred years ago, after a four-hour long feast, a bride was presented with a large cake of *hardbake*, which, when cut, released tiny live birds.

WEDDING CAKE ARCHITECTURE

Just as architectural styles have lent ideas to cake decorators, so too have cake decorating styles had an influence upon architecture. Until the 1950s, Russian architects designed buildings in a highly decorated and lacy style, known in the West as wedding cake.

This style was once adopted by an American sea captain who at the time of his wedding was unable to give his bride a decorated cake. Many years later, to make up for her disappointment, he built her a large two-storey house with elaborate outside decorating. The house still stands in Kennebunk, Maine. It is now a tourist attraction.

WEDDING CAKE DESIGN SINCE 1900

The early years of this century were memorable for their extravagance and romance, both of which were enjoyed to the extreme at fashionable weddings.

With the death of Queen Victoria, many of the restraints of her reign also passed away. Wedding fashions became softer, more feminine and so did wedding cake designs. Creams and ivories were the most popular colours for wedding dresses, while the wedding cake stood out as a stately white monument.

Only members of high society or royalty were able to afford a multi-tiered wedding cake. The rest of the empire had to satisfy themselves with a single layer adorned with special mementos, which towered above the cake to create the impression of height.

Orange blossoms were the most popular flowers for cakes. But the more intricate rose was fast moving up to take over this position. Roses were more often moulded as closed buds and usually appeared in small clusters.

Wedding bouquets measuring up to two-feet across were not unusual up until the First World War. They were made up of a lavish confection of flowers, greenery and trailing ribbons. Nor was it unusual for four or six bridesmaids, as well as the bride and the bride's mother to each carry their own hanging-garden bouquet. Flowers were everywhere.

Weddings were enormous family affairs and every woman attending displayed her own floral tribute in the form of a heavily laden hat. The wider the brim and the more numerous the flowers combined in the decoration, the better.

A smaller version of the wedding bouquet was often duplicated on the wedding cake. But this was an expensive exercise and not everyone could afford to have their cake professionally iced.

During World War I everything about weddings—as about life—became smaller and simpler. Dresses became practical outfits which could be used again. Flowers became far less prominent

and wedding cakes less ornate. But with simplicity came a desire for change. The world was no longer the same.

One change reflected in wedding cake decoration after the War was the introduction of a much wider range of flowers. Lilies of the valley, orchids and gardenias were some of the new moulded varieties which began to appear as confectioners became more adventurous. It seemed everyone had suddenly been made aware of their environment and the beauty of simple things such as a cluster of dainty buds became much more appreciated.

THE ROARING '20s

The 1920s were characterised by the belief that 'anything goes'. The more individual the better. Individuality in both wedding cake and wedding dress design was achieved in the cut more than with the trimmings. Cakes were cut to produce decorated shapes instead of the traditional square. Bells were one of the most popular shapes. Horseshoes were also a favourite.

White was still the most common colour for icing and sugar decorations, although other ornaments added a touch of silver elegance.

Colour was to become an important feature of cake decorating from the late 1920s, when both the bride and the bridesmaids moved away from whites, ivories and silver for their dresses and began to enjoy pastels. Blue became the most popular dress colour for the wedding party–brides recalled the old superstition: 'Marry in blue, you will always be true'. All-over-pink was the most common deviation from white for wedding cake icing.

HOLLYWOOD AND THE 1930s

The 1930s saw the influence of Hollywood, even as far afield as Britain and Australia. Every bride wanted to look and feel like a movie star as she posed for photographs. With the Hollywood wedding came informality. Open house parties after a private wedding ceremony were popular among the social set. The joint-cutting of the wedding cake by the bride and groom became one of the few wedding traditions retained.

Because of the attention given to them, cake decorations became more dramatic and overstated. Shades of colour and large flowers surrounded by extensive piped work were popular, as were two, three, or even four tiered designs.

Large trailing bouquets, however, became a thing of the past. Instead, brides carried casual sheaves of gladioli, lilies, white roses, narcissi, violets or azaleas.

Victorian posies of real, silk or shiny cellophane flowers were being seen in bouquets and cake decorations by 1939.

In 1937, the heart-shaped or 'sweetheart' neckline appeared and wedding cakes were cut in shapes to match. Especially popular was the joined heart design, which brought back the tradition of one cake for the bride and another for the groom.

Another development in 1937 was *plastic*-icing, which became popular in Australia not only for coating but also for decorated borders. The greatest advantage of plastic-icing was that it remained soft for long periods. Wedding cakes could be prepared a few months in advance and the bride could still be assured of piercing the layers when it came time to cut the cake. The more elaborate tube work and moulded sugar decorations were still done in royal icing.

Stronger pinks, greens and light mauves became popular colours for both cakes and bridesmaids in the late 1930s.

By then, even the most intricate flowers, such as carnations, were being moulded for cakes. But more often brides preferred their flowers to be small, often closed buds. Flowers appeared in tight bunches, combined with delicate lattice and lacework, ribbons and tulle.

Everything, including formal weddings, came to a standstill with the outbreak of the Second World War. Wedding dates had to be set at the drop of a telegram and ceremonies performed in a mad dash during a three day leave. There was no time to plan elaborate wedding dresses or to have rich fruit cakes iced with sugar decoration. Even if time could be found, sugar itself was an extremely rare and precious commodity.

Any decoration appearing on wedding cakes during or immediately after the War was in the form of fabric or moulded bread flowers. Fabric flowers were one of the few luxury items unrationed for the duration.

BREAD-DOUGH CREATIONS

Hand-moulded and painted bread-flowers were just as adaptable and just as beautiful as sugar-decorations for wedding cakes. The idea of moulded bread creations dates back many hundreds of years but the art has been practised by very few after the turn of this century, until the necessities of war brought it back into fashion.

Bread-dough has been shaped to create delicate flowers, jewellery, wall plaques, filigree trims and more. Bread-dough jewellery was one of the only forms of adornment many early Australians could afford. The only tools required to produce a practical necklace, earrings and brooch were fresh bread, water, a good pair of hands and some paint.

When the Second World War broke out, it was an easy matter to adapt floral bread-dough techniques to suit wedding cake decoration. Some examples of this artwork can still be found today.

A POST-WAR RETURN TO TRADITION

Once the War was over and rationing had come to an end, brides set about re-establishing the full social wedding with all the trimmings, including a multi-tiered cake.
Queen Elizabeth II's marriage in 1947 rekindled many of the old ways. White gowns, large bouquets in long trailing designs, large bridal parties and a large wedding cake all became popular as other brides followed the royal style.

Elaborate sugar decorations which the bride could proudly show-off to her children and grandchildren became essential in the 1950s, when couples first began requesting photographs be taken as they cut their wedding cake.

Throughout this decade, Australian and English homes were flooded with a wave of 'how to decorate' books, which added to the variety of wedding cake ideas and put beautifully extravagant designs and decorations within the grasp of everyone.

A notable feature of wedding cakes in the 1950s and 1960s was ornate centrepieces, including miniature brides and grooms made from icing or plastic. Other icing creations included miniature churches, houses, birds, butterflies, shoes and scenes, as well as an extensive array of flowers of every size and shape. Brides often removed the ornaments before the cake was cut and kept them as souvenirs.

Since the 1950s people have realised that cake decoration is within the grasp of everyone. The industry is now booming. Classes have become common and design possibilities again extended. The work being done by professional organisations is beyond anything achieved in the past. Amateur work, as we see from the number of awards given to hobby-decorators at shows, is often of an equal standard.

"Wilt thou have this woman to thy wedded wife,
To live together after God's ordinance in the Holy estate of matrimony?"

ARRIAGE

ven though the concept of marriage is universal, no one has yet come up with a definite answer to the question of why people first chose to wed. However, it is generally accepted that the evolution of marriage went something like this:

The very first form of mating between people was seasonal pairing, similar to that found in some animal species. Evidence indicates that a human mating season existed each year around the month of June. But it is not known whether male and female pairs remained together for life, or simply for the duration of each mating season.

THE BEGINNING OF COHABITATION

The beginning of cohabitation between primitive men and women (in cave-man times, 500,000 years ago) came about when the males of our species asserted their superior strength and captured a woman for their own. This woman then became known among the other cave-dwellers as a particular man's property and so was no longer considered 'fair-game'. During the early days of its prevalence, *marriage by capture* was the only process by which a man could establish an indisputable claim to the sole possession of a woman.

MARRIAGE BY CAPTURE

According to a nineteenth century writer, a picture of marriage by capture among primitive tribes would have looked something like this:

> *"An unmarried male would look around until he had discovered a woman who did not fall short of his standards of feminine worth. But, once such an object was found, it would never occur to him to approach his choice with softened smiles or words of love. Nor would he think to make friendly overtures to her people for the satisfaction of his passions. To adopt either of these courses would be to forfeit his own self-respect.*

> *Instead, he would spend a brief time making preparations for his new wife. Then he would spy for a few days upon the victim and her guardians to determine the time when it would be most safe to creep under cover of night to her camp-fire and bear her off, stupefied with terror, or stunned with blows.*

> *The bride for her part would have been anticipating the time when her turn to be taken would come—her feelings probably a combination of mingled hope and horror.*

If upon seizure she decided her companion was repugnant, all she could do was breathe a silent prayer her male relatives would hear of her plight in time to overtake and rescue her from her assailant. If she was to betray her alarm and disgust by an exclamation likely to arouse the surrounding sleepers, her would-be husband would raise a murderous club and with a single blow to the head secure the assent of silence. Once she was laid senseless, the bridegroom would take a firm hold of his bride's ankles and drag her away over the broken ground to his home."

As the race of man developed, this system of marriage by capture remained for many centuries. Civilised races in the Mediterranean, Africa and Asia are known to have practised it, as did people in Biblical times.

Several cases of marriage by capture are cited in the Bible. The tribe of Benjamin procured wives by massacring the inhabitants of Jabez-Gilead and capturing four hundred of their virgins. This same tribe also carried off women during a feast near Bethel. And there is the story of how the Israelites vanquished the Midiantites so that they could acquire their cattle, women and children.

——— ENGLAND'S VERSION OF MARRIAGE BY CAPTURE ———

Marriage by capture was practised in a similar fashion in England during early Anglo-Saxon times. One of the few differences was that the horse was introduced to assist in the get-away.

A Saxon bachelor ready for marriage would gather enough friends together to protect him from disturbances during his project and to overcome any resistance that the relatives of the chosen lady might offer. Then they would set forth, more like men on a hunting trip than guests at a wedding.

After coming across a suitable wife, the bridegroom would leave his friends hidden in the surrounding woods and approach her when she was alone. When face to face, he would bluntly declare his intentions and order the lady to surrender. If she rejected him, he would catch her hands and bind them with a cord before throwing her across the back of his horse.

The groom would be lucky indeed if he encountered no opposition from the lady, and also managed to carry her off at full gallop beyond the boundaries of her village without having to battle with male members of her family. In reality, he seldom arrived home without having to fight for his prize. A bride's father was always furious at the loss of a valuable unmarried daughter. To prevent any unplanned weddings he, his brothers and his sons remained always prepared to fight.

It was when there was threat of such a fight that the hidden friends of the suitor had an opportunity to gain prestige in the service of their friend. They would lay-in-wait prepared for battle and make the first surprise attack upon the pursuing party. If all went well they would manage to hold off the bride's family until the groom had enough time to get himself and his prize to safety.

The results of these battles were various. Sometimes the victorious father regained his daughter, while her lover was left wounded or dead on the field. Sometimes the pursuers would allow the groom to get home with his fair booty, but only if he and his friends had fought manfully and at the end of the battle promised to give the father generous compensation.

Eventually, it became obvious to the groom, his co-conspirators and the bride's male relatives that a much easier way to settle the future of young couples would be to forego the dramas of capture, and the risks of the battle and simply negotiate on the generous compensation. So gradually developed *Marriage by Purchase*.

MARRIAGE BY PURCHASE

Marriage by purchase became a complicated and law-binding procedure during the Saxon reign, when legislators deemed it worthwhile to lay down precise rules for the selling of daughters and the buying of wives, so as to prevent haggling.

But, even when laws were laid down, few chosen wives had a say in their suitors, not even ladies of the court. The Count of Flanders' daughter, Lady Matilda, a woman of very illustrious descent who married William the Conqueror, found her initial refusals of his marriage proposals were of no avail. After being turned down more than once, William forced his way into the Lady's palace, knocked her down, beat and abused her. After which, it is said, she changed her mind and happily consented to the marriage because she knew she would have a powerful husband.

WEDDING AUCTIONS

One of the most workable systems of wife purchase existed among the Babylonians. Twice a year all girls of marriageable age were assembled in a space before the temple and offered for sale to the highest bidder, very much in the manner of our modern *auctions*. The most handsome girls brought large prices and this money was turned over to the more homely girls who had appeared at several auctions and had not been disposed of. The money added to their attraction of course and so every girl ultimately won a husband.

HOW MUCH WAS A BRIDE WORTH?

The amount considered a good price for a bride varied depending upon the wealth of the district. The Navajos of New Mexico, for example, considered twelve horses an exorbitant price for a wife and paid this only when the rank and personal charms of a woman warranted it. The Patagonians, on the other hand, would exchange mares, stallions, silver, ornaments, and trifles for a bride. An average price for one Patagonian woman was three horses, a silver cup, several rich skins and a collection of inexpensive bracelets.

In some parts of Africa, horses were not considered a proper exchange for a woman, but it was perfectly acceptable to barter women for cattle. Other African tribes held an ox and a woman at about the same value. Among the Kaffirs, ten cows was considered a fairly good price, but some brides cost as many as thirty. In Uganda the usual price was four bullocks.

THE ADDITION OF A LITTLE ROMANCE

Romance probably entered courtship when the struggle for mere existence became less pronounced and men and women found time to daydream. This happened at different times in different civilisations, but the Greeks were definitely a romantic lot. Gifts from the bride to the groom and vice-versa played an important part in Greek courtship. The Romans also enjoyed giving and receiving gifts. By the late Middle Ages even the English had picked up the habit. Eventually Medieval England became a very romantic country. Knights went so far as to engrave the initials of their heart's desire, along with their own, on the trunks of trees.

WITH ROMANCE CAME ELOPEMENT

To avoid marrying a man she disliked, or to enable her to marry a man who could not afford the purchase price, a girl had no choice but to elope.

Elopements occurred frequently during the period of marriage by purchase. By the tenth century it had begun to take over as the most common form of wedding. Eventually, the high number of elopements led to parents giving their daughters the right to refuse an offer of marriage. Marriages for love alone slowly became acceptable, all of which lead up to the system of marriage we know today.

IF ALL ELSE FAILED

Before our present system was accepted a few other alternatives were tried out and discarded.

One system attempted to solve the problem of high bridal prices and penniless grooms by allowing the favoured suitor to work for the father of the bride for a given period, at the end of which the maiden would have the say of whether or not she wished the wedding to go ahead. The weakness here is only too obvious. Many a groom toiled for a year or more to the benefit of the bride's family, only to be told at the end of the time that his love had found herself another lover.

Wrestling and fighting were also tried out as a method of determining which males would obtain a wife and which would miss out. In fact, the Greek games were as much a display of courtship as they were competitions of strength among males. Only unmarried females were allowed to watch the Greek games. The young girls could study the participants' naked bodies and choose which they would like as their suitor.

SOME FOLKS PREFERRED TRIAL MARRIAGE

Interestingly, our present custom of living together before marriage goes back much further than most parents think.

Among the early Danes, for example, there existed a curious kind of marriage-contract known as *hand-festing*. According to this custom, it was entirely correct for unmarried people to choose a companion and then live together for one year. If they were still pleased with each

other at the end of that year they remained together for life. But, if they were not happy they separated and were free to make another choice.

We find traces of a custom very similar to this in England in the seventeenth century and in Scotland in the seventeenth and eighteenth centuries. It was known there as *hand-fasting,* or *hand-in-fist.* At the beginning of a set period there was a mutual exchange of rings. At the end of the period, if the couple did not wish to remain together they returned the rings, separated and chose another companion. This custom seems to have been quite common during the reign of Queen Elizabeth I, but had died out by the Victorian era.

Elegio and Ilva Romanin first met on a spring Sunday, while walking in the Italian countryside. The trees were in full bloom, the weather was perfect and, according to Elegio, romance was in the air.

The couple were introduced by two self-appointed match-makers, Elegio's cousin, Gipriano and Ilva's best friend, Olimpia. They courted for two years, then quietly married in a Roman Catholic Church in Pordenone, the town 80 kilometres from Venice, where Ilva lived.

Elegio lived three kilometres outside Pordenone, in Villa Darco. On Saturday, 10 April 1948, the morning of the wedding, he, his family and guests set out to walk the distance to the bride's house. From there a second procession, headed by Ilva, her father and the best man, headed to the old stone church.

"The order of the procession was very important," Elegio says. "The bride and her father must go first. Then it is my turn. I walk with the bridesmaids. Then come my godparents. Then all of the family of the bride and finally my own family. No one is allowed to walk out of order. This is the tradition."

The procession numbered about forty in total. The only two people who did not join in were the mothers of the bride and groom.

"Our mothers stayed at home to prepare for the wedding feast," Ilva explains. "And Elegio's mother remained especially so that there would be someone waiting to greet us when we arrived at our new home."

Ilva's wedding dress was a town frock with a matching coat, both of which she made herself.

"When we married, Italy was still getting over the war," she recalls. "Everyone was poor. People wore their best clothes to a wedding. Very few brides could afford to have a white wedding dress. And, anyway, there was not a lot of material available for sewing."

"The wedding ceremony, performed by Ilva's uncle, Monseigneur Lozer, lasted about one hour. The highlight," Ilva says, "was the singing and organ music."

"My friend, a woman from Pordenone, played and led the singing and all the guests joined in so that their voices echoed around the stone walls. The sound was very beautiful."

As the bride and groom left the church, guests threw rice, confetti and sugar-coated almonds over their heads.

"Almonds are connected with all Italian weddings and anniversaries. They are said to bring good luck to the couple. After their golden wedding anniversary, Ilva's parents sent small packets of golden almonds to relatives around the world. We still have ours here," Elegio says, going to look for them.

The Romanin's wedding feast was held at the home of Elegio's parents, where the bride and groom planned to live for the first year of their marriage.

As the wedding party completed the three kilometre walk to Villa Darco, the villagers welcomed them by spreading ribbons across an archway decorated with flowers.

"The words Villa Pulsa, welcome, were written across the main ribbon," Ilva says. "As I came to the first house, I was given a pair of scissors so that I could cut the decorations and make a way through. Everyone was watching and as the ribbons fell they cheered."

Elegio's mother and her friends had prepared a four-course lunch for the guests, commencing with chicken soup and finishing with sweet biscuits, rather than a wedding cake.

But the party itself did not end after the last course. The bride and groom farewelled their last guests about eleven at night. After ten hours of music and dancing.

As the couple made their way to bed, Elegio's mother gave them a timely warning. Guests had earlier in the day placed five bells discreetly beneath their mattress. This was an old custom. But, on this occasion, those friends waiting outside in the night air to hear bells ringing were sadly disappointed.

A few months after their wedding, Elegio announced to Ilva that he had begun to make plans for them both to move to Australia. The news came as a complete surprise. "I had no idea where Australia was!" Ilva laughs.

However, over thirty years, three children and three holidays back to Italy later, she admits she has no regrets about the marriage, or the move.

RADITIONS

he tradition of a wedding cake dates back to pre-Christian religious and social regulations, so too do almost all the other enjoyable customs observed at a modern social wedding.

As long ago as the ancient Mesopotamians, in 2700 BC, the head male in each household possessed a ring engraved with the family seal. No contract, including a wedding contract, could be entered into unless the terms were written upon soft clay tablets and the ring seals of both parties applied to bind the commitment.

As soon as the wedding celebrations had concluded a Mesopotamian groom's first task was to have his own ring made with his family seal inscribed.

Later, the wealthiest Mesopotamians sealed their wedding contracts with a solid bar of silver or gold. The bar would be broken into two, with half going to the family of the bride and half to the family of the groom. When the wedding contract was fulfilled the pieces would be reunited and presented to the married couple.

The ancient Romans copied this custom and passed it across Europe and England. During the passage of time the tradition was modified until it developed into the custom, practised world wide today, of the bride and groom presenting each other with a gold or silver wedding ring.

THE FIRST CHRISTIAN WEDDING RING

A wedding ring was first introduced among the Jewish people in the eighth century. Its use replaced the custom of handing the bride a small coin, regarded as a promissory note symbolising the husband's ability to meet all future financial obligations towards his wife.

Pope Nicholas in the year eight hundred formally acknowledged the Christian use of a wedding ring when he stated it represented a pledge of fidelity as binding as a sacred covenant. But Christian puritans during the Reformation (which began in 1517) repudiated its use, claiming it was a pagan custom based on non-Christian superstitious contrivances. Rings did not come back into fashion for Roman Catholics until almost three hundred years later.

Other civilisations also developed their own traditions of a wedding ring, but for many different reasons. In ancient Egypt wedding rings became a sign of bondage—a symbolic reminder of the days of marriage by capture, when men would bind the hands and feet of the woman they chose as their wife in order to escape with her quickly and quietly. Even today

some Egyptian women living in villages along the Nile valley wear heavy brass or silver wedding rings around their ankles rather than on their fingers.

Among some primitive races, when a man married a woman he would tie a rope of reeds around her waist in the belief that the ring formed a magic circle, shackling their bodies together so that his spirit could enter the bride's soul. Once the man's spirit had gained possession, the couple would be held together by supernatural forces, whose control could never be broken.

THE ENGAGEMENT RING

In early civilisations, engagement rings were far more common than wedding rings.

Marriages in Roman times were arranged by parents when couples were still very young children. An engagement ring then, as now, indicated to others that a man or woman had been pledged and so was no longer 'on the market'.

It is believed that a Roman emperor, Maximilian I, was the first person to present his love with an engagement ring containing a diamond. The ring was presented to Mary of Burgundy, whom Maximilian married in 1477.

According to Roman superstition, the diamond's sparkle originated in the alchemist's fires of love. So it came to be considered the only stone suitable for engagement rings, portending love and happiness throughout life.

The Romans also believed gold was the perfect metal for engagement and wedding rings because of its beauty, lustre and its resistance to rusting. The lustre of gold was said to have come from the sun, the most powerful heavenly body. It is because of its association with the power of the sun, that gold came to be considered the earth's most precious metal.

THE ENGAGEMENT PARTY

The custom of throwing an engagement party developed much later than the concept of betrothal itself. But, by the twentieth century it was a widely accepted and much enjoyed social occasion.

On the English island of Guernsey, about one hundred years ago, the parents of a bride and groom combined to give an engagement party, known locally as a *flouncing*. All their relatives and friends were invited and were expected to form a circle around the room so that the groom's father could lead the bride from one person to the next, introducing her to his relatives, while the bride's father did the same with the groom, only moving in the opposite direction. Once the introductions were complete, rings were exchanged publicly and the couple were considered betrothed. This ceremony was almost as binding as actual marriage. Once rings were exchanged there was no going back.

THE BRIDAL SHOWER

Legend has it that many years ago in Holland a beautiful girl gave her heart to a miller—a young fellow who had little in worldly goods, but who everyone loved because of his kindness. He was poor because he gave his bread and flour to the needy.

The girl's father forbade the marriage and told his daughter that, if she married the poor miller, she could not have the dowry he had placed aside for her. Instead, he had selected a man he considered a satisfactory husband—a farmer who owned one hundred pigs.

The people for whom the miller made bread heard of his plight and were sorry, so they got together and talked the matter over: 'Too bad the beautiful girl would lose her dowry. Couldn't we do something about it?' They did not have much money, but each one thought of a gift he or she could contribute so that the miller and his love could marry and set up their own home.

When everything was gathered together, they came to the girl's home in a gay procession. One with an old Dutch vase. One with plates for the kitchen shelves. One with linen made on a hand-loom at home. One with a shiny new pot. They showered her with these gifts, providing the bride with a finer dowry than her father ever could.

Some years later an English woman heard of a friend who was about to be married and decided that the only gift she could afford to give was too slight an offering to express the good wishes that she felt. Remembering the story of the Dutch 'shower' and knowing that there were other friends who felt the same way as she did, she called them together and suggested that they present their gifts at the same time.

The 'shower' which they gave was so successful and caused so much comment in fashionable circles that it became definitely established as a social custom and has remained so ever since.

THE BUCK'S NIGHT OUT

The tradition of a buck's final night out as a single man is said to date back to ancient Greece. Greek males traditionally held a party in honour of the groom before his wedding. Wives and girlfriends were excluded from the invitations, but prostitutes were encouraged to attend. The party, which often lasted all night, was known as the *men's mess*.

WEARING WHITE

For almost as long as people have worn clothes, white has been the colour for brides. Most people believe it was originally worn because it was the colour associated with the vestal virgins of ancient Greece, but possibly the tradition goes back even further than this. Pagan civilisations older than the ancient Greeks considered white the safest colour for brides because it was the only colour with the power to deter evil spirits.

There have been, however, periods in history when a special white wedding dress was not considered practical or appropriate.

In the Middle Ages and through to the Renaissance, some brides dressed in lavish fabrics woven from silver and gold thread, or in rich materials, the colour of their family crest. Poorer folk considered their wedding the one day in their adult life they could afford to spend-up on a new 'Sunday-best' outfit–which usually consisted of a practical brown walking skirt and jacket, a white blouse, possibly trimmed with lace, button-up boots, gloves and a bonnet.

In the late eighteenth century the white wedding dress made a return to fashion. Brides then liked to give the impression they were ladies of leisure, wealthy enough to afford lace and flounces. Usually, after the wedding, the bridal gown was adapted to be worn as a ballgown for the season.

SOMETHING OLD, SOMETHING NEW...

The old English rhyme which states every bride should wear
something old, something new, something borrowed, something blue,

is of nineteenth century origin and is one of the best known of all wedding superstitions. Many modern brides still faithfully stick to these principles. Originally, a fifth line, *and a lucky penny in her shoe,* finished the poem. But, for some unknown reason, this last token, implying a desire for wealth, was dropped over time.

In this rhyme, something old and something new symbolises the bride giving up her old life and embarking upon a new one. Something borrowed ensures she will not forsake her friends after her marriage. The reference to something blue is believed to have come from the ancient Israelites, who held blue to be the colour of purity, love and fidelity. They also associated it with magical good health. Brides in the early eighteenth century believed if they married in blue their love would always be true.

Today, brides often include a blue lovers' knot in a seam of their wedding dress, or wear a blue garter. The first lovers' knot was fashioned by Danish fingers and was said to symbolise the binding nature of marriage vows. When introduced to Britain it was quickly adopted as a symbol of faithfulness and sentimental devotion. The lovers' knot became one of the most popular insignias for love in pre-Norman England.

THE BRIDE'S VEIL

Today, a bride's veil is a much shorter and lighter version of the wedding mantle worn in ancient times. Traditionally, in both ancient European and Asian wedding ceremonies, brides were kept hidden from their husbands beneath layers of clothing until the marriage blessings had been bestowed. Ancient Greek brides always wore veils of yellow over their white gowns because yellow was considered a lucky colour which pleased the gods. Roman and Chinese brides both wore red veils over white gowns, probably for similar reasons.

In some countries, wedding veils are folded away after the marriage ceremony and kept to be worn again by the bride as a shroud when she is buried.

FLOWERS AND THE BOUQUET

Flowers at a wedding have always been associated with fertility. Traditionally, Greek brides carried orange blossoms as their bouquet because the orange tree is one of the most fertile of plants, blooming and reproducing in all seasons. In Roman times brides preferred to carry red roses, which were dedicated to Venus, the goddess of love.

Other flowers have been fashionable for wedding bouquets at various times because of their association with certain emotions. Violets are traditionally associated with faithfulness, the snowdrop with hope, the daisy with innocence and the lily with purity. The honeysuckle is said to symbolise happiness. But the rose and the forget-me-not have always been considered the most romantic of flowers.

FLOWERGIRLS

Flowergirls first joined the wedding procession in Medieval England. The first flowergirls were simply children from the village who would accompany a bride and her family on their way to meet the groom. As the children danced around the bride they would scatter handfuls of wheat and other grain–symbols of fruitfulness and prosperity–along her path in the hope she and her husband would be blessed with many children.

Our modern tradition of throwing rice over the heads of the bride and groom as they leave the church is believed to have been derived from the old custom of flowergirls scattering wheat or other grains. Rice is used today simply because most homes have some in the pantry and so it is convenient to take to a wedding.

BRIDESMAIDS AND GROOMSMEN

Both bridesmaids and groomsmen first became involved in marriage ceremonies during the time of marriage by capture.

The groom's men were warriors he selected to assist him defend himself from members of the bride's family if they put up strong opposition to the marriage–which they almost always did unless the price was right.

In Medieval times the role of the male attendants was reversed. By then brides were simply purchased without the drama of the capture and inevitable fight. It was the role of the bridesmen to ensure no harm came to this valuable piece of property until after all transactions had been settled to the bride's father's satisfaction. Usually, the head men in a family would bring the bride in a solemn procession to the groom's house, but they would not hand her over until both sides had agreed upon her worth.

Bridesmaids served a similar role to groomsmen. During the time of marriage by capture, when a young girl reached marriageable age a number of female guards were assigned to her in the hope that their presence would prevent a warrior from kidnapping her before her father had arranged a suitable marriage.

GIVING AWAY THE BRIDE

This concept is believed to be as old as the idea of marriage itself. Certainly during the time of marriage by purchase fathers 'gave away' their daughters for a price. By the time the Greek civilisation had developed, it was customary for a bridegroom to go to the house of his betrothed and formally ask her father for her hand in marriage. If the bride's father agreed, he would walk his daughter to the house of the groom where both families would begin to make plans for the wedding ceremony and feast.

THROWING THE BRIDE'S GARTER AND BOUQUET

Fun-loving French wedding guests came up with the idea of the bride throwing her garter and her bouquet to guests at the end of a wedding. It was believed that whoever caught the garter would have one year's good luck. Whoever caught the bouquet would be the next person to marry. When the idea of the bride throwing her garter caught on in England, the French, to stay one step ahead, actually had the groom remove the bride's stocking and throw it to the guests. Today, most brides stick to removing and throwing only their garter, possibly because of the popularity of pantyhose!

MAKING A TOAST

Eating from the same dish and drinking from the same cup is considered a binding act in many cultures and this custom has been incorporated into many wedding ceremonies. Today, when guests drink a toast to the bride and groom they are symbolising the bond of friendship between everyone gathered.

Five or more toasts are customarily made at a formal wedding:
–to the bride and bridegroom
–to the bridesmaids
–to the parents of the bride
–to the parents of the groom
–and again to the bride and groom before they cut the cake.

A response, followed by a second drink, is made after each toast.

MUSIC

Music of some sort–the melody of a single instrument, the strains of a martial band, the humorous din of pots and pans–was the universal accompaniment to a wedding in olden times.

When Charles II was King of England (from 1660 to 1685) he encouraged musicians and guests to continue celebrating a wedding long after the bride and groom had been put to bed. Wedding parties often lasted all night. A bride not roused on the morning after her wedding by the musicians was said to have been shown disrespect.

And what a noise those musicians liked to make to rouse her. Our English ancestors relied

chiefly upon the drum to beat out a jolly tune. In Scotland they preferred another noisy contrivance, the bagpipes, to waken newlyweds.

In country areas the fiddler of the district was the chief, if not sole, musician at the bridal party for a wedding in a poor family. But the poor in London could not even afford a fiddler. Instead, they relied upon friends who delighted in producing a festive sound from hollow bones, cleavers, tongs, shovels, saucepan lids and tin kettles containing stones. Noise of this sort won the name *rough music*.

GAMES

Outside the circles of the religious Puritans, no marriage was ever celebrated by our ancestors in the seventeenth century without dancing, competitions and friendly games.

One of the favourite games was jousting. Knights would ride at full gallop towards poles or straw dummies, in an attempt to retrieve a handkerchief or some other small possession belonging to the bride. Their reward was the honour of presenting the trifle back to the lady and receiving her eternal friendship. Sometimes, when two knights wished to obtain one lady's hand in marriage, they would joust against each other, the winner receiving the bride as his prize.

A less dangerous, yet just as serious game played at weddings by poorer folk in Feudal England was a race to the festal house immediately after the ceremony was complete. The main object of the contest was to give the cook timely notice to dish up the banquet. The winner was rewarded with the first serving.

THE HONEYMOON

The word *honeymoon* originated from the custom of drinking mead (a wine made from honey considered an aphrodisiac) for one month (a moon) after Greek and Roman weddings. The concoction was a very powerful mixture and did not always achieve the desired effect. It is said the scourge of Europe, Attila the Hun, drank so much mead during his wedding feast that he died before he had time to enjoy his honeymoon.

Honeymoons were introduced into Christian wedding tradition because they were seen to serve a useful purpose. Christian religion states that a marriage is not binding until it has been consummated. In order to ensure the marriage act was performed satisfactorily, early Christians would lock newlyweds in a room for a period up to or, if necessary, exceeding a month.

LEAP YEAR BRIDES

Why is it that custom dictates ladies can propose to their beau only in a leap year? When was this 'rule' established? We were unable to find an answer to either question, yet it is a fact that a law was enacted in Scotland in 1288 which stated:

"It is statut and ordaint that during the rein of her maist blissit Mageste, for ilk yeare known as lepe

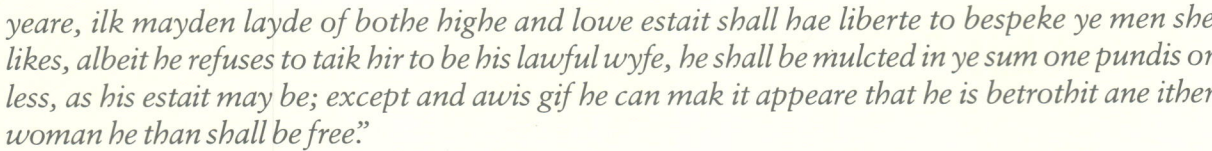

yeare, ilk mayden layde of bothe highe and lowe estait shall hae liberte to bespeke ye men she likes, albeit he refuses to taik hir to be his lawful wyfe, he shall be mulcted in ye sum one pundis or less, as his estait may be; except and awis gif he can mak it appeare that he is betrothit ane ither woman he than shall be free."

A few years later a similar law was passed in France and in the fifteenth century the custom was legalised in Genoa and Florence, Italy.

Sometime after these laws were enacted it was decreed that should a gentleman be uncivil enough to decline a lady's proposal she had the right to demand from him a new silk dress. But the gentleman only had to fulfil this demand if the lady was wearing a scarlet petticoat when her proposal was turned down.

One author advised bachelors in the leap year of 1856:

"After careful consideration of the various dangers arising from the feminine folklore that will beset me and all other bachelors during the next twelve months, I am inclined to think that whenever we see a young lady 'in full fig' with a scarlet petticoat coming down the street we should show our best discretion by turning and running away."

ACCORDING TO THE IRISH

The Irish claim the tradition of leap year proposals arose in their country. According to a *tall* Irish fable, the custom originated with Saint Patrick, who was once told by Saint Bridget that a mutiny had broken out in her nunnery because some ladies claimed the right to 'pop the question' (a rather strange thing for nuns to want to do). To quieten things down, Saint Patrick said he would concede them the right every seventh year. After hearing this, Saint Bridget threw her arms around Saint Patrick's neck and exclaimed "Arrah, Patrick, jewel I daurn't go back to the girls wid such a proposal. Make it one year in four." Saint Patrick replied: "Bridget, acushla, squeeze me that way agin, an' I'll give ye leap year, the longest of the lot." Saint Bridget, upon hearing this, popped the question to Saint Patrick himself, who, of course, could not marry; so he patched up the difficulty as best he could with a kiss and a silk gown.

"Will you promise to love him, cherish him, honour and protect him?"

RIBAL CUSTOMS

ompared to some native wedding traditions, European marriages have always been gentle and predictable affairs. Native brides could not always be sure their grooms would make it through the festivities and, even if they did, they were not always in the best of health.

The Macusis tribe in British Guiana had a fairly typical wedding ceremony for their race. According to Macusis tradition, before a young man was allowed to choose a wife he had to prove to tribal elders that he was a *man* and could do a man's work. A potential groom could display his worthiness by either suffering the infliction of wounds in his flesh without once flinching, or by allowing himself to be sewn-up in a hammock full of fire ants. Once manhood had been established, all that was left was for the youth to show he was capable of working to support a family. This was comparatively simple considering all he had already endured. Young men would usually be requested to clear a space in the rain forest and plant it with *cassava,* then bring in as much fish and game as possible, all within a set time. Needless to say, not all Guiana males chose to marry.

Among the Bororo tribe of South Africa, every young man who wished to be considered eligible for marriage must have killed either five wild pigs or one jaguar. Men who had killed five jaguars were eligible for two wives.

If a man was a member of the Wapokomo of East Africa he could marry only after he had killed a crocodile and given some of its flesh to his chosen woman to eat.

In many head-hunting tribes in both Africa and Asia tradition stated that no man could marry before he had first procured at least one human head as a token of his valour.

Wedding customs of the Koryak tribe of South Africa once dictated that to be eligible for marriage a young man must be a good hunter and fisherman and also capable of doing everything necessary within the household. Once capability in these areas had been determined, the groom's father-in-law would go to the rain forest and fell the thickest, tallest tree he could find. The groom was accepted into the family only if he could drag the tree through the forest to the door of his father-in-law's house.

Even after this test of endurance the groom's path to marital bliss was not clear. On the eve of the wedding the bride's parents would attack the bridegroom with sticks. When they had beat him enough, everyone else in the family was invited to have a turn. The groom was expected to show himself as a man by receiving the floggings with fortitude and without any sign of resistance.

Some Arab tribes in upper Egypt had a similar custom of whipping the bridegroom to test his strength. If a groom wished to be considered worthy as a husband he was expected to receive his whipping with an expression of enjoyment.

Some African tribes had quite gruesome customs when it came to making a choice between marriage suitors. In one tribe, if two men wished to marry the same woman but she could not make a choice between them, the woman had a knife tied to each of her arms so that the blade protruded below her elbows. She would then sit on a log with the two men sitting either side of her and raise her arms so that, as she lent forward, the knives would be pressed into their thighs. The suitor who best endured this trial of endurance won the bride.

In other cases, where women were scarce, men were expected to fight for their right to marry. Among Australian Aboriginal tribes living along the Hunter River, if a man wished to marry he would wait until men and women were sitting together around a fire and then he would throw his boomerang into the circle. If another man threw the boomerang back, they would fight for the right to any of the single women. If there was no challenge the man was free to step in and make his choice of a wife.

—————————— NOT ALL CUSTOMS WERE GRUESOME ——————————

Whenever an alliance was desired among the members of some North American Indian tribes, all the would-be groom had to do was weave a belt or some other gift and give it to the parents of the girl he had chosen. If they approved of his craftsmanship, preparations for the wedding would commence at once.

In the traditional marriage ceremony of the Ulu Langat Sakai tribe of the Malay Peninsula, relatives on both sides would sit around an anthill while the bride or her father questioned the bridegroom:

> *Are you clever with the blow-pipe?*
> *Can you fell trees well?*
> *Are you a good climber?*
> *Do you smoke cigarettes? (a later innovation).*

If the groom answered yes to each of these questions he was allowed to give a cigarette to the bride and light one himself. Then he would chase the bride around the anthill three times. If he succeeded in catching her the ceremony would be complete and they were considered married. But, if the bridegroom failed to catch his bride, the marriage would be abandoned.

Cows played an important role at weddings in Zulu country. The price for a bride among the Zulu was about twenty good-sized cows and, as if to highlight the equality of this swap, marriages were usually held outside the entrance to the kraal, with the bride and the animals being presented together.

The traditional Zulu wedding ceremony was short and sweet. The bride advanced with great dignity to the entrance of the kraal and fell upon her knees to receive a necklace of beads from

her suitor. After he had placed the beads around her neck, the groom raised his bride to her feet and placed a band of white beads, symbolic of his belief in her virginity, around her waist. Then they entered their hut and remained a little while alone. During these few minutes the bride was expected to decide if she would take this man *for better or for worse*. If the decision was favourable they emerged hand-in-hand and their friends assembled outside would strike up a song of congratulations. Then everyone participated in a community dance. If the decision was not favourable the girl emerged alone, the guests dispersed and the marriage did not take place.

AN ORDEAL OF FIRE

In Albania, fire was long regarded as one of life's sacred symbols and, therefore, it played a large part in marriage ceremonies. Albanian males traditionally abducted their wives-to-be. When a girl was captured she was taken to the assailant's home and placed before the fireplace. A huge fire was built and she was given a large pair of fire-tongs. For three full days she was obliged to stand tending the fire, her head bowed, her hands always grasping the tongs. She could not speak. She could not even rest. Whatever food or drink she needed was brought to her. At the end of this ordeal she was considered married and she could take her place in the household.

A heavy belt took the place of a wedding ring among the Albanians. After the three-day fire-ritual, the belt was placed around the bride's waist and she preserved it throughout her life.

As recently as 1925, travellers reported that, even when a bride and groom were married by a priest, they would still go through this age-old fire custom and would not consider themselves actually married until it had been completed.

On the Marquesas Islands, in the north-eastern corner of Polynesia, no man could marry without the consent of his mother, but he could bring home many girls to stay with him for the night. Often a mother would take a particular liking to one of these girls and so call a family council after the two had gone to bed. If the family agreed with the mother regarding the girl's suitability, they determined to arrange a wedding.

Early the next morning, just before dawn and well before the young couple awoke; all the women of the household would arouse them with screams and shrieks. They beat their breasts, cut themselves with shells, cried loudly *Aue! Aue!* Neighbours would rush in to see who had died and the youth and his girl would run from their room in terror. Then the mother, the grandmother and all other women in the house would chant the praises of the girl, singing of her beauty and wailing that they could not possibly let her go. They would demand that the son appreciate her superiority over other girls, until the son, covered with shame, would be forced to ask the girl to stay with him.

If the girl's parents had no objection to the young man, she would remain in his house and they would be considered married.

Among some native races it was always the woman rather than the man who selected the partner for marriage.

Unmarried men and women from Indian tribes in Paraguay would wander from village to village during the marriage season. In each village dances would be performed on four successive evenings. At the end of each dance the females could choose a partner to stay with them the night. The choice on the fourth night was said to be decisive. If a man was selected by a woman on the fourth night he was expected to stay with her for life.

In the time of the Old Testament, a Jewish Rabbi watched on as a young man said to his bride: "Behold, thou art betrothed to me with this ring, in accordance with the laws of Moses and Israel." In an almost identical ceremony in Melbourne, 2000 years later, John Aarons married his wife Rachael, using the exact same words.

The fundamentals of the orthodox Jewish wedding ceremony have not changed with time.

"A Jewish marriage is a contract," John says. "The laws governing the contract were originally passed down, by word of mouth, from Moses to his followers until they were written in the Torah (the five books of Moses) for us to follow.

"Because the laws were originally recorded as oral history, there are now many interpretations of their exact meaning. But, basically, they exist to remind us that life is not a bowl of cherries. Every life has a certain duration. We will not be here forever, so we must make the best of everything that comes our way while we have the opportunity. Especially, we should make the best of marriage."

John and Rae Aarons were married on 19 January 1932, at the St. Kilda synagogue. As luck would have it, it was the hottest day recorded in 40 years.

"We actually met in London," Rae recalls. "John's father was the manager of a store across the road from my family home."

Unbeknown to each other, as teenagers both John and Rae moved with their families to St. Kilda, Melbourne. Their first Australian meeting was on a tennis court.

What happened, according to John, was that Rae accused him of pinching a court she and her friends had booked for the afternoon. There was no easy solution to the problem, except to share the court. Love blossomed from there.

Rae and John's engagement lasted two years. "We, that is both our families, including aunts, uncles and cousins, all went out to the movies to celebrate the announcement," Rae recalls. "The picture was The Jazz Singer with Al Jolson, one of the first talking movies. It was a real treat."

Rae and John were married two years after their engagement.

On the morning of the wedding, Rae stood beneath a large canopy bedecked with flowers. She was wearing a white wedding dress of Chantilly lace with satin bound inserts and a full-length tulle veil, which covered her head completely. Between prayers, she greeted guests and received their congratulations.

The tradition of covering the bride's head and face with a veil originated with the marriage of Rebecca and Isaac in the Old Testament. Rebecca completely covered her head when she met Isaac for the first time.

After the marriage of another Old Testament couple, Jacob and Leah, it became the custom that only the bridegroom could cover the head of the bride for the wedding. You see, Jacob had wanted to marry a beautiful woman called Rachael, but on his wedding day he was tricked into marrying her sister, Leah, because of the veil. John Aarons had no such worries he was marrying the wrong bride.

All Jewish weddings are performed beneath a Chuppah or canopy. "This represents John's home, which will soon also become my home," Rae says. "Both John and I were led to the Chuppah by our families, who then stood all around us, along with our friends and elders of the synagogue."

"I could not see where I was going because of the veil, so I was led by my mother in a circle around John seven times." ("Almost everything in the Jewish religion is done seven times, because of the seven days of creation," John explains.)

Rae adds: "The circle signifies my building a fence around my husband, behind which he will be safe from all evil and harm."

Then the Rabbi bestowed seven blessings upon the couple, a wedding ring was placed on Rae's right hand and wine was drank from a cup, then, as the completion to the ceremony, John broke a wine glass with his foot to remind everyone of the destruction of the Jewish Temple and the ultimate destruction of life.

"It was only after this that John lifted my veil and I could see my husband and friends again."

Because the day John and Rae chose for their wedding was so hot, few of their 150 guests danced to the four-piece orchestra, but the wedding feast and three tiered wedding cake, decorated with white royal icing and pink roses matching the bride and bridesmaid's bouquet, was enjoyed by all.

USTOMS

ust as every culture has developed individual practices which make their wedding day celebrations unique and special to them, there is a striking similarity in wedding customs world wide.

A WEDDING IN OLD JAPAN

There were many obstacles to prevent the course of true love from running smooth in old Japan.

Class distinctions were especially numerous and acted as powerful inhibitors if either a bride or groom desired to marry a person of lower rank. To prevent embarrassment arising from a declined proposal, the Japanese came up with a simple way for a young girl's parents to show they considered a particular youth a suitable match for their daughter. Once a young man had fixed his sights upon a maiden, he declared his passion by placing a branch of a certain shrub near the door of her home. If the branch was neglected and died he knew his suit was rejected. If it was watered and flourished he knew his love was also being encouraged to flourish.

Once their engagement was announced, Japanese maidens were expected to blacken their teeth to declare their new status and to make themselves unattractive to other suitors.

The ceremonial delivery of presents from the family of the groom to the bride was once one of the most important parts of the Japanese wedding ceremony. The bride, in turn, would give these presents to her own parents to acknowledge the kindness they had shown her throughout her life. As thanks, her parents would provide her with a handsome trousseau, which was carried, along with the bride, to the home of the bridegroom on the day of the wedding and displayed to all the guests.

A colourful procession of family, friends and villagers accompanied the bride from her home to that of her betrothed. But she did not join in the customary fun or dancing. A bride traditionally arrived locked in a palanquin (a covered litter carried by four or six men) and was not released until the groom received the key to the palanquin from his father-in-law.

According to an age-old custom, two men always ran in front of the palanquin waving red cloth. The cloth was believed to ward off evil influences and protect the bride until she was safely united with her husband.

When the procession finally reached the bridegroom's house, everyone was invited in for a feast and to view the trousseau.

Japanese brides traditionally dress in white for their wedding ceremony, to signify their purity. They once were also covered from head to foot in a white veil. The veil was kept after the wedding and used again as the bride's shroud.

In ancient Japan, the groom and all the wedding guests dressed for the occasion in ceremonial clothing or rich gold-bordered gowns.

MARRIAGE CHINESE STYLE

Ancient Chinese weddings had many similarities to those of the Japanese. Again, the bride was locked in a sedan chair, along with her trousseau, and carried to her future home, where both she and the key were assigned to the bridegroom. But it is unique to the Chinese that the bride was expected to show the utmost modesty and bashfulness, as if she had a natural aversion to marriage, until the wedding celebrations were over. This behaviour went on regardless of whether or not the bride approved of her husband and was happy to marry.

Everything connected with a Chinese wedding was once regulated by a code of behaviour, from which no one dared to depart. The code was specific in its detail. Among other things it stated that a bride, her sisters and her lady friends must lament for a period of not more than one month and not less than ten days preceding a wedding. During the lamentations the bride would frequently declare that the thought of leaving her parents was more than she could bear; death itself was preferable.

The lamentations ended on the wedding day when the bride said goodbye to her own family for the last time and headed for her new home, where a wedding breakfast awaited her.

Another rule, according to the code of behaviour, was that tables must be arranged at the east and west ends of the dining hall in the bridegroom's house on the morning of the wedding. Food was placed on these tables. Another table, the nearest to the door, could hold only four wine cups, known as *uniting cups,* from which the bride and groom drank.

When the bride arrived at this feast, she was immediately placed on the back of a female servant and carried over a slow charcoal fire. As she and her bearer crossed the fire another servant passed a tray containing chopsticks, rice and nuts over her head.

Only after all this was the groom allowed to lift the bride's red silk veil, so that the couple might see each other for the first time.

The Chinese wedding ceremony was then performed beneath a sacred umbrella, which was believed to prevent evil from falling upon the heads of the bride and groom.

On the night of the wedding, a second feast was held so that the friends and neighbours of the groom's family could come to 'view' the bride. Any of these guests had the privilege of asking the bride a riddle, which she was obliged to answer. Whenever her answer was incorrect, the bride paid for her mistakes by giving the guest a serving of small cakes.

As with the Chinese wedding, Jewish wedding ceremonies are performed beneath a special canopy, called a *chuppah,* which is said to represent the new home the couple is about to build for themselves. A Jewish wedding does not have to be held in a synagogue, it can be held anywhere as long as the chuppah has been erected.

There are two separate processions in a Jewish wedding, one led by the bride, the other by the groom. To start, the bridegroom stands beneath the canopy and waits for the bride's friends and family to bring her to him. When she arrives, the bride circles the groom seven times. Then the rabbi greets them and recites a series of seven special prayers, praising God and his creations.

The crucial moment in the ceremony is when the bridegroom takes the ring and places it on the forefinger of the bride's right hand, while making a declaration of his intentions in Hebrew. The offering and acceptance of the ring constitutes the union between the couple.

Everyone in the wedding party then shares wine from a cup which, once it is empty, is placed on the ground before the groom. As the groom smashes the cup with his foot, everyone is reminded of the destruction of the Jewish temple in Jerusalem. The broken cup is also a reminder that marriage vows can be destroyed just as easily unless they are protected.

It is traditional for the bride and groom to fast on their wedding day until after the service, so they and their guests especially enjoy the feast which follows every marriage.

── RUSSIAN WEDDING GAMES ──

The old Russian attitude to marriage was similar to the Chinese in that they too liked to give the impression brides would avoid their wedding day if it were possible. Brides in Russia were traditionally crowned with a garland of wormwood, said to represent the bitterness of the married state.

As a modern Russian bride leaves the church, hops rather than rice are thrown over her head, in the hope she will prove to be as fertile as this plant.

The chief ceremony at a Siberian wedding was once a game of hide and seek.

Long ago, the people of Siberia lived in large tents, with many compartments separated by hanging curtains of reindeer skin. Some homes contained as many as twenty-six compartments, all arranged in a circle around an open space in the centre. At a wedding, guests would crowd together in this central space to share food and to dance. Early in the celebrations the bride and groom would be brought forth for everyone to see but, before anyone had time to voice their congratulations, the bride would feign shyness and dart away into the first compartment. Frightened at the thought of losing his bride, the groom would quickly follow, but by the time he had arrived the bride had doubtlessly escaped into the second compartment. Again he would follow, but his progress was considerably impeded by women who

endeavoured to prevent him from catching his bride. The women would beat the groom with willow rods as he rushed along in hot pursuit. As the bride gained greater distance, other women joined in and attempted to trip him up, or to entangle him in the reindeer skins so that he became lost and ran the wrong way. Through all this the groom rushed on, at least if he was determined not to fail in his objective. Finally, in the last compartment the couple were again united and the celebrations commenced.

A HINDU FAMILY WEDDING

At a Hindu wedding the bride and groom marry their partner's whole family rather than just each other, so every one of their close relatives is given a role to perform during the ceremony.

The groom, rather than the bride, takes the lead role at a Hindu wedding. The bride is hidden at the start. She does not appear until after the groom has made a grand entrance, dressed in his best clothes, carrying flowers and wearing a garland given to him by his parents.

It is the mother of the bride's job to greet the groom. Then, as members of both families watch, she shows him five symbols which represent the tasks expected of him in marriage. After studying the symbols, the groom must confirm for everyone that he is ready to undertake these responsibilities.

Other symbolic rites at a Hindu wedding include the bride and groom removing their shoes so that their feet can be washed; the passing of the groom's original garland to his best man, and an exchange of fresh garlands by the bride and groom.

Once all this has been completed, the right hands of the bride and groom are clasped together and covered with a white scarf. Then a rope is placed around their necks to bind them as one. Linked like this, the groom leads the bride three times around a fire and the bride leads the groom in the same circle a fourth time. The circling symbolises they will care for each other during the four stages of life.

A SIMPLE QUAKER MARRIAGE

Today, about the simplest wedding in the world is the marriage of two Quakers. There is no minister or priest, no bridesmaids, best man or flowergirls at a Quaker wedding—this religion teaches that everyone plays an equal role in the sight of God. Nor does the bride wear any special clothing or carry flowers. When two Quakers wish to marry they simply attend their normal religious service. Then, when they feel ready to speak, they stand up and say to the assembly:

> *Friends, I, John take my friend Amy to be my wife (or husband), promising with God's help to be unto her (or him) a faithful and loving husband (or wife) so long as we both on earth shall live.*

After the meeting, every member of the congregation signs the marriage register as a witness to this act.

FEASTING AT A GREEK WEDDING

The Greeks traditionally have the longest wedding celebrations. In many regions, festivities start the night before the wedding, when the groom is made welcome into his new family at a dinner given by the bride's parents. Then, after dinner he is taken off by his male friends to enjoy his last night as a single man.

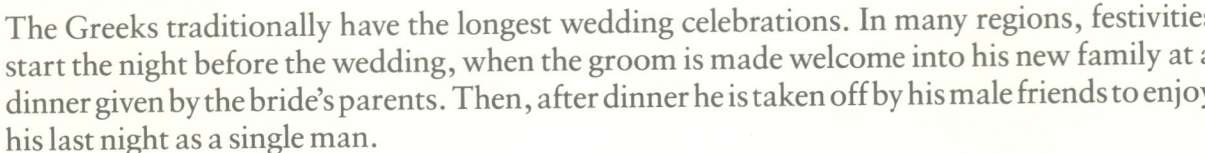

There are two separate religious ceremonies in a Greek wedding. The first, the betrothal, was once held when the couple first announced their engagement, but today both are generally performed together on the day of the wedding. Both ceremonies are religiously binding and both can be dissolved only by a priest.

At the end of the Greek ceremony, crowns of orange blossoms are placed on the heads of the bride and groom. Then they and the rest of the bridal party, link hands and perform a religious dance around the table where the service was held.

Before leaving, everyone kisses the orange blossom crowns, which the priest takes and keeps in the church for forty days. When the forty days are up the bride and groom collect their crowns, often framing them above their bed as a memento of this happy day.

A LOCK OF MAIDEN'S HAIR

Marriage arrangements in Afghanistan were once about the world's simplest. Today they have become one of the most complicated.

Many hundreds of years ago, the unmarried women of this country went about unveiled. All a young man had to do, if he wished to secure a maiden as his wife, was cut off a lock of her hair, or throw a veil over her head. Then, once her parents had been informed and a suitable price had been arranged, the damsel was his.

Now, marriages are usually arranged when children are very young. The parents take care of all the negotiations and no man is allowed to see or speak with his betrothed until after the wedding.

A DUTCHMAN'S METHOD OF COURTSHIP

Traditional Dutch courtship arrangements were possibly the most open to misinterpretation.

In some parts of Holland, when a youth took a fancy to a girl, he stood at the door of her house and asked her parents for a match to light his pipe. If he repeated the visit, again asking for a match, the young lady's parents had no doubt in their minds he intended to propose marriage to their daughter. On the young man's third visit they informed him whether his suit was viewed with favour, or not. If they were willing to accept him as a son-in-law they asked him inside, where, at last, he received his match to light his pipe. Then, the elders retired, leaving the young couple alone.

Often the intended bride had no knowledge of the goings-on until this stage, so she was forced to quickly make up her mind whether she wished to be courted. If not, she simply told the smitten young man to make for the door.

WELSH AND IRISH TRADITIONS

The Welsh and Irish even today like to play up the old custom of marriage by capture at their weddings.

Among the Irish hill-villagers, a marriage is considered quite a tame affair and scarcely legal unless the bride attempts to escape and the bridegroom overtakes and captures her.

It is an old custom in Cardiganshire, Wales, for the relatives of the bride to seize her as she reaches the church door and ride off with her. The bridegroom and his party must follow in pursuit. When the groom's party overtakes the bride she is gently handed over and everyone goes back to the church. If someone else besides the groom catches the bride it is said this person will also marry within the year.

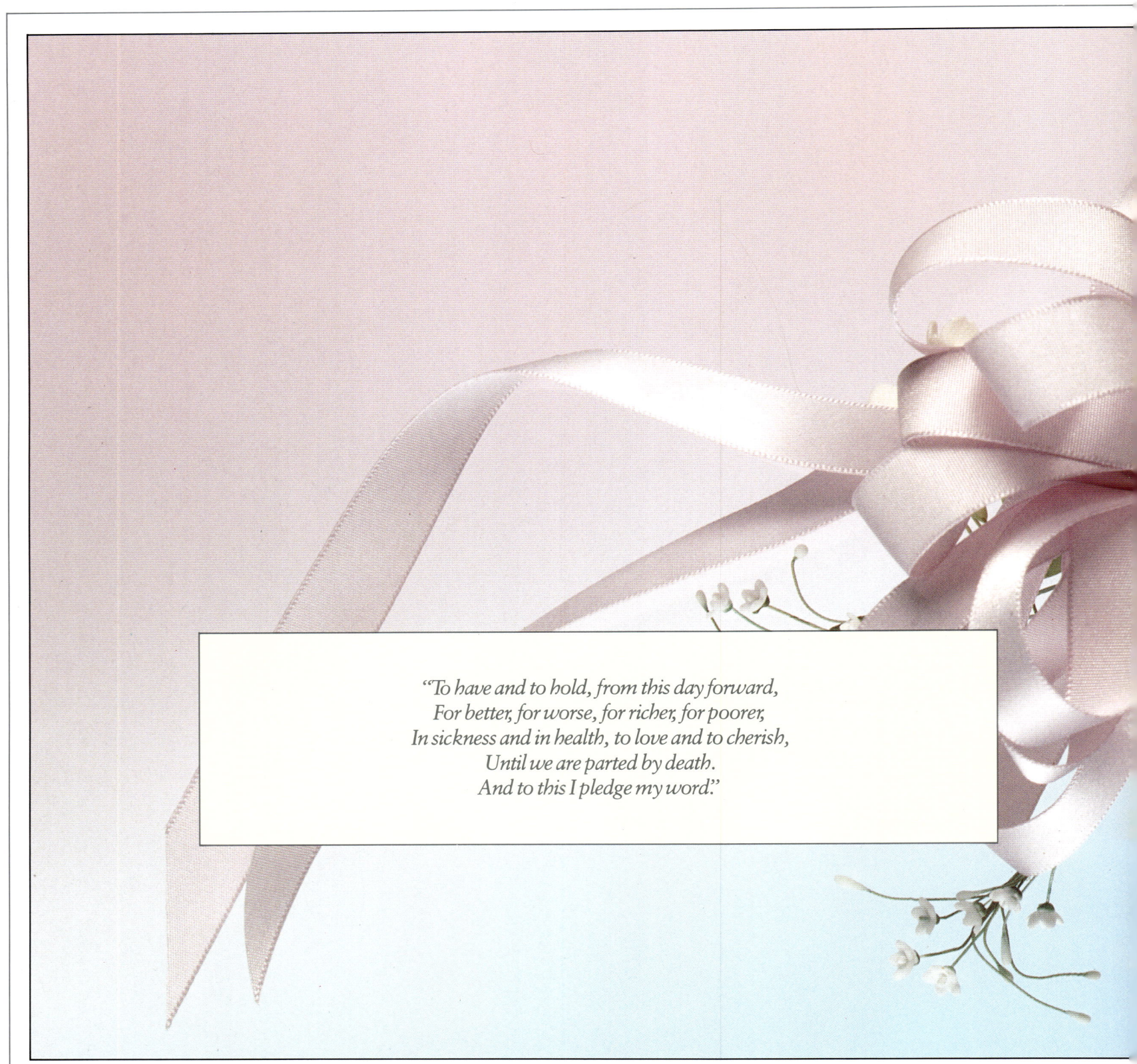

"To have and to hold, from this day forward,
For better, for worse, for richer, for poorer,
In sickness and in health, to love and to cherish,
Until we are parted by death.
And to this I pledge my word."

ARRIAGE VOWS

arriage is simply a promise made by two people to each other, witnessed by a priest or other official and by friends and relatives of the bride and groom.

Elizabeth Mary, will you take Antony John to be your lawful wedded husband? Will you promise to love him, cherish him, honour and protect him?

The word wedding comes from the Anglo-Saxon word *wed*, meaning to pledge. Originally, the pledge was a financial one–the groom paid the father of the bride for the right to marry his daughter. Today the pledge is made when the bride and groom promise to "love, honour and (sometimes) obey."

There have been many different versions of marriage vows exchanged at wedding ceremonies. Modern couples, marrying in a church today, are likely to repeat a promise such as this:

> *"I Michael, take you Catherine to be my wife*
> *According to God's holy ordinance:*
> *To have and to hold*
> *From this day forward,*
> *For better, for worse,*
> *For richer, for poorer,*
> *In sickness and in health,*
> *To love and to cherish,*
> *Until we are parted by death.*
> *And to this I pledge my word."*

Or the priest may ask them:

> *"Catherine, will you take Michael to be your husband,*
> *To live together as God has ordained*
> *In the holy state of matrimony?*
> *Will you love him, cherish him,*
> *Honour and protect him,*
> *In sickness and in health;*
> *And, forsaking all others*
> *be faithful to him, as long as you both shall live?"*

After this the rings are exchanged with these or similar words:

"With this ring I wed you,
With my body I worship you;
With all that I am and all that I have I honour you."

Finally, the union is recognised when the priest states:

"Those whom God has joined together
Let no man put asunder."

— OUR WEDDING VOWS ORIGINATED WITH THE SAXONS —

A very similar version to our wedding vows was used by Anglo Saxon brides and grooms as long ago as the year 800 AD.

Then, a bride was taken by her husband:

"For fairer or fouler, For better or worse, For richer or poorer."

She in turn promised to be "Debonair and buxon in bed and at board." *Debonair* at the time was taken to mean good-humoured. A promise to be *buxon* was a pledge to be pliant and yielding.

As we can see, vows over the past one thousand years have changed very little, except for a little modernisation. The greatest allowance to today's bride being, of course, the abolition of the word *obey*.

From 1549, brides marrying in English churches were asked:

"Wilt thou obey him (their husbands)
and serve him
Love, honour and keep him,
in sickness and in health?"

To which they were obliged to reply they would do all of these things "in bed and at board until death us do part."

Things did not really change until this century when, in March of 1914, the English daily newspapers received a flood of letters from emancipated females regarding their objection to the use of *obey* in modern marriage ceremonies, even though by then its emphasis had been much toned down.

Just as many letters were sent to the newspapers in reply, stating that the marriage vows as they stood were appropriate and applicable. The use of *obey* was justified because of its link with a statement in the New Testament:

"Wives, submit yourself unto your own husband, as unto the Lord."
Ephesians 5:22

The dispute was to last more than fifty years. In the 1960s, marriage vows still contained the word obey. Then, a groom was asked:

> *"Wilt thou have this woman to thy wedded wife,*
> *To live together after God's ordinance in the Holy estate of matrimony?*
> *Wilt thou love her, comfort her,*
> *Honour and keep her,*
> *In sickness and in health;*
> *And forsaking all others,*
> *Keep thee only unto her*
> *So long as ye both shall live?"*

While the bride was asked:

> *"Wilt thou have this man to thy wedded husband,*
> *To live together after God's ordinance in the Holy estate of matrimony?*
> *Wilt thou obey him and serve him,*
> *Love, honour and keep him,*
> *In sickness and in health;*
> *And forsaking all others,*
> *Keep thee only unto him*
> *So long as ye both shall live?"*

But slowly, over the next ten years, vows with and without the disputed word became acceptable.

The debate was finally put an end to when Prince Charles married Lady Diana Spencer on 29 July 1981. At this marriage *obey* was for the first time given the royal boot.

Both Prince Charles and Lady Diana vowed they would live together:

> *"For better, for worse,*
> *For richer, for poorer,*
> *In sickness and in health,*
> *To love and to cherish,*
> *Till death us do part according to God's holy law."*

WILT THOU BE LOYAL?

Loyalty, rather then obedience, is the promise most often asked of both bride and groom.

In the Jewish wedding ceremony, the groom promises his bride loyalty and support using these, or similar, words:

> *"Be thou my wife, according to the laws of Moses and of Israel, I faithfully promise that*
> *I will be a true husband unto thee. I will honour and cherish thee. I will work for thee.*

I will protect and support thee. I will provide all that is necessary for thy due sustenance, even as it beseemeth a Jewish husband to do. I also take upon myself all such further obligations for thy maintenance, during thy lifetime, as are prescribed by our religious statutes."

In Tahiti the bride and groom's loyalty is tested with the question:

"Wilt thou cast away thy husband (or wife)?"

To which they must answer "No!"

Even the Quakers, who have the simplest wedding vows, find room to include an assurance of faithfulness, with words similar to these:

"Friends, I take this my friend, Maree,
to be my wife, promising, through divine assistance to be unto her a long and faithful husband, until it shall please the Lord to separate us."

A curious custom at both traditional Chinese and Hindu marriages hands the responsibility of the marriage vows to the fathers of the bride and groom, rather than to the couple themselves.

The Chinese once made their wedding pledge in letters, the words for which were passed down from generation to generation.

When a Chinese father received a letter asking if his daughter was free to marry, he was obliged to reply:

> *"The choice that you design to make of my daughter to become the wife of your son shows me that you esteem my poor and cold family more than it deserves. My daughter is coarse and stupid and I have not had the talent to bring her up well; yet I shall nevertheless glory in obeying you on this occasion."*

The groom's father then wrote a similar letter about the unworthiness of his son, after which all that was left to do was send the bridal procession to the home of the groom and enjoy the wedding feast.

Although Hindu marriage vows are made in front of the Brahmins (priests), the bride and groom take a back seat to their fathers until their marriage promises have been made.

The bride's father makes the first promise when he says to the groom's father:

> *"I give you for your son my beautiful virgin daughter; accept her therefore."*

To which the bridegroom's father replies:

> *"With my hand, with my voice and with my body I joyfully accept thy daughter for my son, and religiously receive her among my own kindred."*

Then the bride's father says to the Brahmins:

> *"Oh Brahmins, to this youth, learned in the Vedas, I give my daughter, dressed in gay apparel and adorned with gems."*

The marriage is blessed when the priests reply: *"So let it be."*

Monica and Steve Karavasillis were married at Saint Ignatius Church in Melbourne, on Saturday 15 March 1986, at 1pm. They were also married at Trinity Church on the same day at 2pm. "Our marriage was a well blessed affair," Monica now jokes.

The reason for the double ceremony was that Monica belongs to the Catholic religion and Steve to the Greek Orthodox. "It was all a bit of a jumbled combination of two cultures, but somehow it fitted together on the day," Steve sums up.

For both ceremonies, Monica wore a white wedding dress of French lace with beading. The design, her own, featured a plunged waistline with a full skirt falling from the hips. "For luck, I added a blue garter and I also carried a borrowed basket of flowers. But I forgot about wearing something old. Even my underwear was brand new." Steve wore black tails in contrast to the white dinner suits and white gowns with pink trim worn by the three groomsmen and bridesmaids.

"Our guests were invited to attend either the Catholic or the Greek ceremony, but the majority of them decided to attend both," Monica says. "Which was really nice considering they both lasted almost an hour." "The two ceremonies were very different," Steve recalls. "The Catholic one was more formal, a mass with singing and organ music. Greek weddings involve the people more. Especially the best man. His job is very important. He places crowns of white flowers upon the head of the bride and the groom and then exchanges these three times. Then he takes the wedding rings, after they have been blessed and he exchanges these three times. Then we all form a procession around the altar, circling three times."

Steve explains the number three is significant because it represents the three arms of the cross.

After the two services, Steve, Monica and their guests enjoyed a wedding breakfast of Greek and Australian foods.

"We started off with Greek dips, but the main courses were more international," Monica explains. "It was a bit difficult to cater for everyone's taste."

"Our wedding cake was cut at the end of the meal and served with coffee. It was something really special. The lace and flowers on the icing were made to match the lace on my dress and my bouquet. There were orchids, roses and small groups of other tiny flowers. And the lacework extended out around the edges. We still have one tier. We're saving it for the christening of our first baby."

Con and Maria Karavasillis, Steve's parents, recall that their wedding service in Thessalonika, northern Greece, was similar to their son's. But events leading up to the wedding day were vastly different.

"We started the celebrations one week before the wedding day," Maria recalls, speaking in Greek with Steve doing the translation.

"Our wedding day was a Sunday, the fifth of June 1958. For one week before this day we were not allowed to see each other. We spent the time with our families and friends. On the Wednesday my parents put on a party for all my friends to attend."

"A young boy and girl went around to everyone's house, with a bottle of Ouzo, offering them a drink and an invitation to come and see my trousseau. Everything that I had worked on for my new home was taken out of my glory-box and put on show. All the women came to see."

Maria's family and friends continued to celebrate with parties and dancing until the following Saturday. Con's family were doing the same.

Then, on the Sunday, everyone prepared for a big celebration. But Con's first responsibility was to go to Maria's home to accompany her to the church for the mass.

"I walked to her house with my best man. But when I arrived she wasn't ready. She was sitting in her wedding dress, but she had no shoes on and her feet were in a baking dish full of rice, coins, sweet almonds and lollies. And her head was covered with a towel."

Before Maria could leave for her wedding, guests insisted upon breaking a loaf of sweet-bread over her head into the baking dish. Then the contents of the dish were tossed into the air for people to catch. "The contents were all symbolic," Maria explains. "The coins were for a strong relationship. The lollies represented a sweet life. The bread was for fertility. It was said the girls who caught the bread would dream of their own husbands that night, if they placed pieces beneath their pillow."

Maria was again given a loaf of bread at the end of the wedding ceremony, which she tucked under her left arm. Con's arm was then snugly tucked under her right arm and together they marched off to their new home, where the party was to be held.

"When we arrived at the house, Con's mother was waiting for us, with two spoonfuls of honey, which she gave us to eat as we entered, so that our lives would always be sweet," Maria recalls with Con nodding in agreement.

119

TIQUETTE

oday, there is really no such thing as *wedding etiquette* – a *correct way* for things to be done. A modern wedding can be whatever the bride and groom decide to make it. So can a modern wedding cake.

Whilst the majority of couples still stick to the professionally adorned multi-tiered wedding cake, many couples, either as a result of national custom, or simply of personal preference, choose an alternative style of wedding cake.

Since the 1970's, newly married couples at their wedding breakfast have been known to cut a light and delicate sponge covered only with cream; a heavy chocolate gateau; or a *croquembouche* – a conical structure of profiteroles filled with custard cream and coated in caramelised sugar.

For those couples who wish to stick to tradition, as least as far as their wedding cake is concerned, here are a few tips.

The cake itself can be as large or small as you like to make it. Ideally, it should allow for the guests present at the wedding breakfast with a tier remaining, to be cut on the couple's first anniversary; upon the christening of the first child; or at some other anniversary or milestone. It should be a rich moist fruit cake symbolic of fertility and the desire for a plentiful harvest.

Whereas the wedding cake was traditionally covered with a white icing, many brides now choose the cream and ivory colours popular in bridal gowns today. A cake coloured to match the bridesmaids' dresses can also be an attractive feature. Beneath the icing, there should always be at least a light layer of marzipan – simply because marzipan was an important part of early wedding cakes.

Wedding cakes are usually displayed as the centrepiece of the bridal table or, if they are particularly large, they may be given their own table, set in a prominent position where everyone can see the masterpiece.

The cake is cut just before the bride departs to dress in her going-away outfit or, if she has decided not to change, before coffee is served.

Usually a special knife decorated with a flower or ribbon will have been set aside for the cutting. The bride and groom stand when they are ready (this is a sign for everyone to check that their glasses are full) and the bride places her right hand on the handle of the knife. The groom then covers her hand with his own. They insert the knife together, making two cuts in the form of a

wedge, after a spokesperson has made the final toast "to the bride and groom." If the couple wish, this wedge can then be removed from the cake and shared by them.

There is normally no reply to this last toast, but if the couple wish they may return the salute by proclaiming "to all our friends."

It is traditional at military weddings for the cake to be cut with a sword, but today most couples leave this bit of added grandeur to colonels, majors and members of the royal family.

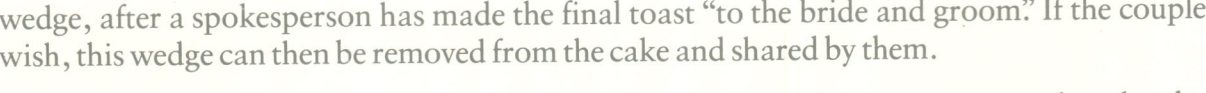

After the first slice of cake has been eaten by the bride and groom, the remainder is taken back to the kitchen and cut and served to guests, who may either eat it immediately or ask for their piece to be wrapped so that they may carry it home.

ANNIVERSARIES TO LOOK FORWARD TO

As well as a piece of cake, married couples have the following presents to look forward to on their wedding anniversaries:

First	Paper	Thirteenth	Lace
Second	Cotton	Fourteenth	Ivory
Third	Leather	Fifteenth	Crystal
Fourth	Silk (or Flowers)	Twentieth	China
Fifth	Wood	Twenty-fifth	Silver
Sixth	Iron	Thirtieth	Pearls
Seventh	Copper	Thirty-fifth	Coral
Eighth	Bronze	Fortieth	Ruby
Ninth	Pottery	Forty-fifth	Sapphire
Tenth	Tin	Fiftieth	Gold
Eleventh	Steel	Fifty-fifth	Emerald
Twelfth	Linen	Sixtieth	Diamond

THE NECESSITY OF A WEDDING CAKE

According to an English publication, *Miss Manners' Guide to Excruciatingly Good Behaviour*, a traditional wedding cake is vital if a marriage is to be a long and successful union.

The forethought and planning required to produce a wedding cake both the bride and groom–and their mothers–can be proud of provides many hurdles for the engaged couple to overcome. Miss Manners believes it is only those couples who learn to conquer hurdles early in their relationship who end up enjoying diamonds sixty years later.

To help engaged couples find marriage a cinch, here is a checklist of hurdles Miss Manners recommends be jumped before the big day:

Six months before the wedding:

"Fight over whether wedding is to be formal or informal.

Fight over size of wedding.
Fight over whether seventy-five people can be considered a small wedding.
Fight over whether wedding cake will consist of fruit or chocolate.
Fight over whether silver and china are a better investment than stereophonic equipment."

Three months before the wedding:

"Fight over whether relatives you do not like should be invited to wedding.
Fight over whether wearing a white wedding dress will be worth enduring the sneers of people who believe these must be accessorised with intact hymens.
Fight over whether the mother of the bridegroom should be forced to wear a type of dress she dislikes in order to be visually paired with the mother of the bride, who finds that style flattering.
Fight over whose mother will decorate the wedding cake."

Two months before the wedding:

"Fight over what money can be found for a catering firm to decorate wedding cake.
Fight over discovery that bridegroom's family has not only exceeded its quota of guests, but has provided a list using initials instead of names and terms such as *and family,* meaning children.
Fight over whether guests' requests to bring their current love interests should be honoured and who is going to tell people that their small children will not be welcome.
Fight over slurs made towards relatives who sent cheap and nasty presents."

One month before the wedding:

"Fight over whether it is the bride or the bride's mother who is at fault because elderly relatives are beginning to complain that their presents have not yet been acknowledged.
Fight over whether roses or scene of a football match will feature on wedding cake.
Fight over whether seating arrangements should be done according to tradition or according to who is speaking to whom."

One week before the wedding:

"Fight over failure of some guests from each side to answer invitations and about who is going to prod whom so as to provide accurate numbers for the caterer.
Fight over how much luggage can be taken on the honeymoon.
Fight over whether a knife or an edge-tool will be used to cut the wedding cake.
Fight over the wisdom of marrying a person now discovered to be short-tempered, stylistically alien to one's own tradition, and completely absorbed in petty detail to the exclusion of any intellectual or romantic activity."

"With this ring I wed you. With my body I worship you;
With all that I am and all that I have I honour you."

128

SUPERSTITIONS

istory has shown there have been few races more superstitious than the British.

Each English, Welsh and Irish county, each Scottish region, has many a folktale to tell about ceremonies, feastdays, flowers, animals, eating, sleeping, work and play.

They have superstitions about the cause of babies, the cause of illness and the cause of dying. There are others about names, numbers, the days of the week, planets, the weather, the four seasons.

But more than any other, the British adhered most strongly to their superstitions regarding courtship, marriage and the thousand and one things which must be done to ensure a wedding day turned out perfectly.

Superstitions relating to weddings vary from county to county. However, here are some which were commonly practised, and not all that long ago!

IDENTIFYING A DESTINED MATE

From a very early age, English children, especially young girls, were given a number of different methods to determine the identity of the person they would marry. One folktale claimed that if an unmarried girl or boy pared an apple without breaking the peel and then threw the peel over their left shoulder it would form the initial letter of the surname of their destined partner.

If the initial was different to that of their own name all was well. But if their initials were the same the marriage would not be one to look forward to. A rhyme from the shire of Cambridge states that for a girl to marry a man with a surname beginning with the same letter as her own would only bring bad luck:

> *Change the name and not the letter*
> *Change for the worse and not the better.*

Grooms also had another guide when it came to making the right choice for their life-long partner: if a woman was fair the British male could expect she would also be foolish. If she was dark she would also prove proud. If she was tall a groom could expect his wife to prove lazy. If she was little, she would also be loud.

If honeysuckle was brought into a house which sheltered a maiden, superstitious mothers were quick to push their daughter towards the altar regardless of the initial of the groom's surname. It was believed in the Middle Ages that honeysuckle caused young girls to have erotic dreams and it was best to marry them quickly before they were led astray.

Another omen which indicated to a household that a wedding should take place was the division of a candlewick. If the mother of a betrothed girl saw a candlewick divide in two as it burned, she believed she had been sent a sign that the marriage should take place immediately. Mothers anxious to move a sluggish fiancé on, or daughters just as anxious to establish their own homes, often doctored the wick of a candle to cause the fateful division to occur.

A superstition which originated in England in the eighteenth century often proved very helpful for young couples unable to obtain parental approval for their marriage. The superstition claimed that when one person dropped something and another picked it up while loudly exclaiming *"Halves!"* the two were obliged to split the object fairly down the middle. If they did not, they could both experience bad luck connected with whatever had been dropped.

When the object happened to be an engagement ring the only way to successfully split it down the middle was for the couple to unite themselves in wedlock.

A crowd would always gather when the word "Halves" was proclaimed, everyone was curious to see what had been lost and what gained. When they saw it was a ring gained, the crowd would accompany the young couple to the house of the maiden and join with them in breaking the news. It was a very strong and stern father who was prepared to defy the whole village when it came to the marriage of his daughter.

————— THE LIKELY OUTCOME OF A UNION —————

There were many superstitions inhibiting a successful marriage in old England. Most originated in feudal times. Among the most important were the time of the year, the time of the month and the day upon which a wedding took place.

The weeks of Lent and the month of May were considered by superstitious Britons to be the two most unlucky times for a wedding. A religious adage from about the tenth century states: *Marry in Lent; marry to repent.*

The luckiest months were March and September, at the end of the harvest. Luck was doubled if the wedding day also coincided with the full moon.

The middle of the week was considered the best time for a marriage. The last three days (including Saturday) were said to be the most unlucky.

By following a simple rhyme, brides could pick their wedding day depending upon their personal desires:

> *Monday for wealth*
> *Tuesday for health*
> *Wednesday the best day of all*
> *Thursday for crosses*
> *Friday for losses*
> *Saturday no luck at all.*

Other bad omens for the future happiness of a bride and groom include thunderstorms and the singing of certain birds.

In Cambridgeshire it was believed that if a thunderstorm struck during a wedding ceremony the couple would have no children.

If a bride heard a raven croaking as she went to the church she would have a large family, but she would have to rear them in poverty.

It was once widely believed throughout England that a lone magpie sighted at any time meant sorrow. Two magpies sighted meant mirth. A sighting of three meant there would soon be a wedding, while the sighting of four meant a birth.

Many nervous British maidens engaged to be married watched sparrows for a sign of the likely outcome of their union. If a betrothed girl saw a sparrow drinking from a puddle by the roadside she knew this meant her future husband would spend too much time in the public houses. If, on the other hand, she saw a sparrow having a dust bath she knew her husband would never mind how dusty or untidy their home became.

To see a chimney-sweep on the way to or from a church was held to be a very lucky omen. So, in the Shire of Fenland, the best man was responsible for giving the local sweep a shilling and the promise of a gallon of beer to ensure he would be waiting at the church door to kiss the bride after the wedding ceremony. It was believed that if a bride was embraced by so dirty a person she would forever after have a horror of dirt and therefore be a clean and tidy housewife.

If a grave was open in the churchyard when a bride arrived for her wedding she would be forced to turn back. An open grave at this time was about the unluckiest omen she could ever face.

An uneven number of wedding guests was also a particularly unlucky omen because it signified one of the guests would die before the year was out.

Black, being the colour of death, has always been avoided at weddings, as once was green because it was the colour of the elves and fairies. In Scotland they went so far as to banish even green vegetables at a wedding feast in case a wee fellow saw his favourite colour and decided to pay the guests a mischievous visit.

During the wedding feast itself, many of the folktales related to the cutting of the wedding cake.

Unmarried guests at a wedding believed if they wished that night to see in a dream the face of the person they were destined to marry all they had to do was push a slice of wedding cake through the wedding ring nine times and then place the nine pieces under their pillow.

According to another folktale, if a wedding ring is mixed with the ingredients of the cake and baked with it, the person who secures the ring in their slice will secure with it good fortune during the ensuing year. Should the possessor be a maiden she will also obtain a suitor and a happy marriage.

In some parts of Lancashire and Cumberland it was customary to put a ring among the ingredients of the cake and to invite the guests in turn to cut a slice. The person who held the knife when it came upon the hidden ring could be sure of happiness for at least one year.

In the Shire of Burnley it was a common practice at weddings to put a wedding ring into a wine jug. Then the wine would be served to the unmarried guests. It was believed the person whose cup contained the ring would be the next of the company to marry.

Burnley brides would also often put a wedding ring and a sixpence into a common flat currant cake. When the wedding was over and the guests were ready to leave, the cake would be broken and distributed among the single women. The one who got the ring in her portion was expected to marry shortly. The one who got the sixpence would die an old maid.

During the seventeenth and eighteenth centuries it became customary in England for the wine to be drunk and the wedding cake broken in the bed chamber of the newly weds, in the presence of all who had assisted in the nuptial rites. During this very public finish to a wedding celebration games would also be played. Among the most popular was the throwing of the bride and groom's stockings. Either the bridal couple would throw their stockings to the surrounding crowd as they reclined in their marriage bed, or with their backs to the bed, the best man and the chief bridesmaid would throw the disgarded stockings at the bride and groom. In the first instance, whoever caught the stockings would be the next to marry, while the later, whoever succeeded in hitting the happy couple would themselves enjoy a happy life.

The marriage of George III to Charlotte of Mecklenburg-Strelitz in the eighteenth century is said to have been the first marriage in England to finish without the joyful uproar of celebration and stocking throwing in the couple's bed chamber.

The Scottish also enjoyed parties in their bedchamber after a wedding, so long as the bed had been made up by a woman with an unweaned child. If anyone else made the wedding bed the marriage would be sure to prove barren.

In the parish of Claybrook in the early eighteenth century a custom prevailed whereby single men would ride for the bride-cake on the day the bride moved into her new home. A pole was

erected in front of the house, three or four feet high and the cake stuck upon the top of it. The moment the bride set out with her belongings from her parents' home a company of young men started off on horseback towards the pole with the object in mind to knock the stick and capture the cake. The man who succeeded was presented his cake by a young damsel and he then had the honour of presenting it to the bride. A party followed. The custom was said to bring good luck both to the bride and to the winner of the race.

In other areas a similar competition was held on foot. Or heavy bars of iron were thrown by all the single men. The winner was the man who managed to come closest to the wedding cake. The closer the toss, the more luck for the winner and for the bride.

The northern counties of England had their own notable way of dealing with wedding cakes. In the East-Riding of Yorkshire, when a bride was on the point of crossing her father's threshold after returning from the church, a plate containing square buns of cake was thrown from an upper storey window of the house, for the purpose of learning whether she would be a happy or wretched wife. If the plate broke when it hit the ground she should be happy; but if it landed unbroken she would not escape injury.

——— ONCE THE WEDDING WAS OVER ———

Superstitions and folktales did not stop after the wedding was over and the couple had retired to bed. The first duty of many British wives on their wedding night was to check for fleas in the bed. It was an unlucky omen if a flea was found. It was believed that the insect had been placed there by a jealous ex-lover. If a flea was found, a quarrel would be sure to follow with accusations of unfaithfulness before the wedding being flung, so the superstition always proved true.

Both pre- and post-marital unfaithfulness, by husband or wife, was a cause for public condemnation in many English villages during Feudal times. Disapproval was expressed by neighbours gathering outside a house and playing rough music on tins and saucepans until the culprit or culprits were forced to leave the district. Neighbours would do the same if a man was accused of wife bashing or parents accused of child bashing. Brides were always on the lookout for a sign that they had been wronged.

Another method, almost as good as flea detecting, to determine faithfulness on a wedding night was to watch the wick of the candle after it had been blown out. If the tip of the wick glowed red everything was well. But if there was no red glow then one of the couple had strayed before the marriage.

For some, presumably unrelated, reason early last century brides used to knit candles into the border of their bed covers to ensure a happy married life.

If a marriage did prove happy there were many unplanned rewards.

In the village of Dunmow in Essex it was the custom as late as the 1930s for blissfully married couples to be presented with a flitch of bacon if, in a year and a day, they could swear that they had not repented of their marriage while either awake or asleep.

Couples would swear to the following poem when applying for their bacon.

"You swear by custom of confession
if ever you made nuptial transgression
Be you either married man or wife
If you have brawls or contentious strife
Or otherwise, at bed or at board
offended each other in deed or word
Or, since, the parish-clerk said Amen
You wish'd yourself unmarried again
or in a twelfth month and a day
Repented not in thought anyway
Be continued true in thought and desire
As when you join'd hand in the quire.
If to these conditions, without all fear
Of your own accord you will freely swear
A whole gammon bacon you shall receive
And bear it hence with love and good leave
For this is our custom at Dunmow well known
Though the pleasure be ours, the bacon's your own.

A FEW GERMAN TALES

The Germans almost, but not quite, rivalled the British when it came to believe in wedding superstitions.

When a German bride set a date for her wedding, she once paid a great deal of attention to the signs of the zodiac. Couples who were foolhardy enough to marry under the sign of Cancer (July), Scorpio (November), Pisces (March) or Libra (October) were said to be asking for trouble. Anyone who married under these signs at that time of the month when the moon was in the wane was asking for double trouble.

For luck, on the day before her wedding, a German bride was expected to be seen walking behind her dowry-cart as it was conveyed to her new home. If she not only walked but also wept all the way she would have the added assurance of knowing she would not shed any tears during her married life.

Before this small procession started out the bride would make doubly sure all her possessions had been packed correctly, especially the spinning-wheel. If the spinning-wheel was placed in the cart with the distaff side facing towards the horses, the bride need have no fear of dying in child-birth.

The sewing of five crosses onto the bed-quilt was another important job performed by German brides to satisfy a superstition. The crosses prevented witches from casting their spells upon the couple while they slept.

Children of the village also had a hand in a German couple's happiness. When an engagement was announced in a village, children would gather together and throw old crockery against the door of the maiden's house; the higher the broken pieces, the more happiness the wedded pair could expect to enjoy together.

In the country, happiness usually depended on healthy farm stock, so a bride would put a hair from every animal in the farmyard inside her shoe on her wedding day. This was believed to cause the flocks and herds belonging to the young couple to increase and flourish.

To be doubly sure of prosperity on a farm, some young couples would eat a soup made up of all kinds of livestock fodder. This must have been an unsavory concoction, but the eating of it was considered to be a small price to pay for good luck, year in year out, with the cows, lambs and pigs.

Town dwellers also had their own superstitions involving a meal prior to a wedding ceremony. In some districts the bride and bridegroom would eat a single bowl of soup together; but they would watch each other carefully as they did so. It was believed whoever ate the last spoonful would be the first of the two to die.

Similarly, if a light went out on the altar before the elevation of the Host during the wedding, a Roman Catholic groom knew he would be the one to leave a sad widow in her old age. If a light was to go out after this part of the service it was the bride who would be the first to depart.

A priest with a head-cold was an even more ominous sign than a flickering candle for a young couple in the prime of life. The Germans believed that if a priest should unfortunately sneeze during a wedding service neither the bride or the groom could expect to survive a year.

SCANDINAVIAN SUPERSTITIONS

Regardless of nationality, as far as superstitions are concerned the responsibility of ensuring a happy union has always fallen largely on the bride.

In olden days in Sweden, when a bride headed for the church she was expected to have her pockets full of scraps of bread which she would give to the poor folk whom she met along the way. For every scrap she handed out, she and her husband could avoid a misfortune later in life. As for the poor receiving the scant meal, they were forced to throw it to the birds. To actually eat the bread would bring wretchedness upon the recipient.

The groom's role in a Swedish wedding was once to guard and protect his future wife from the evil powers of trolls and bad spirits, of whom the Swedes had a strong fear. To do this the bridegroom would sew various strong smelling herbs, such as garlic, chives and rosemary into his clothes. He would also ensure that no member of the bridal party stood at a closed gate, or where crossed roads met, for fear of ill fortune. These locations were favourite spots for gremlins.

Long ago, an offering was made by every bride and groom to the trolls and fairies, so that they would stay away from a wedding party. The offering, in the form of a plate of delicacies, would be placed beneath the charmed tree of the homestead. Traces of this reverence paid to 'the little people' still remains. By tradition, a Swedish bride today puts something from every dish she eats onto a plate and this is given in alms to a poor dependant of the family.

Like the Germans, the Scandinavians also depended on healthy livestock for a prosperous marriage. The role of a Norwegian bride once included milking a cow after she had dressed for her wedding. By doing this she would ensure milk would never be lacking in her life.

To ensure money would be just as plentiful as milk throughout a Norwegian couple's life, brides would wear a silver coin in each of their shoes. If the shoes featured neither buckles nor lace a bride knew that she would produce a large family and have an easy time of child-bearing, in addition to wealth.

The cowsheds and stables were once the first place a Swedish bride and groom visited after their wedding, so that the cattle might thereafter thrive and multiply.

The Swedes, unlike almost all other races, are glad to see rain on their wedding day. She will be a rich woman, they say, upon whose wedding crown the rain falls.

A Swedish bride would always make sure she put her right foot ahead of the foot of the bridegroom when they stood together at the altar, to ensure she and not her husband controlled the money in the household. To prevent the power she thus obtained from going to her head, the mother of the bride always ensured the first thing her daughter ate after the ceremony was a lump of sugar. This guaranteed the bride would maintain a sweet temper towards her husband throughout their life together.

WHO DOMINATES IN RUSSIA?

At Russian weddings silk carpet was spread on the ground in front of the altar and the priest would lead the couple toward this carpet so that they could kneel together and pray after they had made their wedding vows. As the couple walked forward, spectators would watch their steps with great interest. It was believed whoever stepped on to the carpet first would have the mastery of the other throughout their life together.

Another superstition, which still prevails at weddings in some areas of Russia, is a belief that the happiness of a newly-married couple cannot be assured unless all four parents of the bride

and groom are soaked with water from head to foot following the wedding ceremony.

When a marriage takes place in summer this soaking is easily accomplished by ducking both fathers and mothers in the nearest river, but in winter they must face being laid on the ground and rolled in snow.

WHEN TO MARRY AN ITALIAN

The Italians, like the English, once considered Wednesdays to be the best day of the week for a wedding. Mondays, Tuesdays and Thursday were definitely out of the question. It is said Italians who marry on Mondays are sure to go mad; the bride and groom who marry on a Tuesday can expect endless suffering. Thursday, being the witches' combining day, is the evilest day of the week, so couples who marry then can expect just about anything, except happiness.

MAGIC EMBLEMS IN ASIA

The Asians tend to rely on emblems much more than actions to ensure good luck and prosperity throughout their married life.

One of the luckiest emblems in China is a small orange tree heavily laden with fruit and decorated with strings of money. The tree is said to ensure the couple will have a large family with many sons. The family will also enjoy much worldly wealth. For these reasons a tree so decorated always accompanied Chinese brides on their way to their new home.

Chinese grooms once liked to see a *kee-lum,* a fictional four-footed animal, engraved somewhere on the carriage bearing their chosen wife. The *kee-lum* was said to appear in the flesh only when a wise son was born.

Other animals likely to accompany the *kee-lum* included a goose and gander, emblematic of a happy and fruitful life; and a dolphin which symbolised wealth and rank.

In Japan the goose and gander of Chinese fable were substituted with two pheasants, which represented the same wish.

The Japanese fear the misuse of colour more than anything on the days leading up to a wedding. Nothing will induce a betrothed girl to pour tea over a bowl of red rice. If she did so her wedding day would be sure to be wet and gloomy.

Likewise a bride and groom will never wear anything dyed a shade of purple at their wedding, lest their marriage ties be soon loosened. Purple in Japan is the colour most susceptible to fading.

Irene Grant recalls breaking as many Chinese traditions as she kept on her wedding day. "I was married in white instead of red, which is the colour Chinese people associate with luck. We didn't go in for a ten-course wedding feast. We stuck to a simpler three-course meal. And I washed my hair the morning of the wedding–which is about the worst thing any Chinese bride can do."

The Chinese are highly superstitious, Irene explains. They believe luck is almost a tangible thing, which exists, amongst other places, in a person's hair. If a bride washes her hair the morning of her wedding, the Chinese say she is washing her luck away.

The Chinese also believe that when a girl marries she leaves her own family forever and becomes a part of her husband's family. To compensate for the loss, the bride and her parents receive gifts of jewellery and other precious objects from the groom and his parents.

"Because I was marrying an Australian, we felt the custom of passing over presents, in our case, was inappropriate," Irene says. "But it is a tradition many of my relatives and friends in Australia have followed for their weddings."

While the Grants did not stick to these particular Chinese traditions, Andrew Grant is quick to point out they did follow some other popular Chinese customs.

"The wedding invitations, cake boxes and gift envelopes (in which guests place money for the newly weds) were coloured red and all featured the characters for double happiness in Chinese calligraphy. And Irene wore a red silk cheong sam (a traditional Chinese costume) as her going away outfit," he says.

The Grants also kept a traditional Chinese memento of their wedding day. A red silk scarf inscribed with the characters for double happiness was passed around for guests to sign during the reception. The wishes expressed are a mixture of typical Australian and, Irene says, typical Chinese–from "Good on you" to "Eternal happiness."

Because she was born in Australia and was marrying an Australian, Irene included many Australian customs in her wedding, alongside the Chinese. She carried at least six lucky horseshoes, given to her by guests as she walked down the aisle. She wore a blue garter. And she was accompanied by two bridesmaids, dressed in lilac '50s style dresses with hooped petticoats, along with a four-year-old flowergirl, dressed in white.

The wedding, on 12 September 1987, was held at Wesley Uniting Church in Melbourne and the reception at Ripponlea, where both Chinese and Australian food was served. By coincidence, the Church was the same one in which Irene's parents were married in 1954. They were both from Canton but met after moving to Australia.

A highlight of the wedding reception for both Irene and Andrew was the speech-making and cake-cutting ceremony. The bride and groom both made a speech, in English and Chinese, while the bridesmaids and groomsmen had a laugh reading out the telegrams.

The Grants had a three-tiered wedding cake, decorated with roses, violets and small white flowers. The bottom tier of the cake was cut at the reception and the top tier saved to be cut on their first wedding anniversary.

At the end of the night Irene and Andrew congratulated each other on how smoothly the day had gone. They had spent almost two years saving for and planning their wedding. Everything seemed perfect. At least until they said good-bye to their guests. The only thing Andrew had forgotten to do was ask the driver of the wedding car to return to take them to their hotel. So, at the end of an almost perfect day, the couple called a cab and went on their way.

E LOPEMENT

Elopements and illegal marriages were common in England in the Middle Ages. By then rules regarding who could marry whom had become complicated. Marriages could only be conducted in a church. The tax on marriage licences was high and officials did their best to ensure both laws and taxes were met. But it was still possible to find a priest willing to perform a clandestine ceremony, for a price.

Unfrocked priests in the fourteenth and fifteenth centuries conducted many questionable wedding ceremonies outside the Fleet prisons in London, so illegal marriages came to be known as Fleet Weddings.

Couples who could not prove their lineage, couples who wished to avoid the compulsory calling of bans in order to keep their marriage secret, run-away lovers and under-age brides were the people most likely to avail themselves of a Fleet Wedding. But with the passing of the Marriage Act in 1694 this avenue, along with all other forms of illegal marriage in England, was closed.

The Marriage Act assigned the punishment of transportation for fourteen years to any clergyman convicted of officiating at an irregular wedding. Anyone other than a clergyman convicted of solemnising an unlawful marriage was to be pillared, lose his ears and be imprisoned, until the governor saw fit to release him upon the payment of a fine not exceeding fifty pounds. The Act also increased the tax on "every skin, or piece of vellum, or parchment, or sheet, or piece of paper, upon which any licence or certificate of marriage, or any letter of mart shall be engrossed" to five shillings.

However, there was one loophole in the Act of which desperate lovers took advantage. This was a clause which placed all marriages performed in Scotland and beyond the seas (except on islands under English jurisdiction) beyond the operation of this statute.

Scotland, unlike England, was at that time very lax in its marriage laws. No licence whatever was required for a Scottish wedding and weddings could be held at any time, in any place providing certain residential qualifications were observed–namely that a bride must reside in Scotland for a minimum of three weeks prior to or following her marriage.

At first, run-away couples (most of whom were rich brides and poor grooms unable to obtain consent for their union from the bride's father) made their way to Edinburgh to be married. But often this distance proved too great and they were overtaken by a very angry father before the

ring could be hastily exchanged. So the village of Gretna became the most popular spot for unlawful English weddings. Gretna, just over the border from Carlisle, was the most accessible point in Scotland.

The speed at which a marriage ceremony could be conducted upon Gretna Green became legendary. So called 'parsons' would wait about the Green, in the nearest inn, at the blacksmith's forge, or at some other likely spot. When they saw the dust of an approaching horse being pushed to full speed it took no time at all for them to prepare to perform their much sought after service, which itself could be completed in two-minutes flat.

It is said that some of the races to Gretna Green were so near that betting on the contenders, the bride and the groom versus the bride's father and other male relatives, was at even odds among the spectators. Ten minutes gained or lost by the lovers might cause the success or failure of the expedition.

SELF-PROCLAIMED PARSONS

The self-named 'parsons' who performed the Gretna Green marriages had no right to that title at all. They were mere impostors, who were clever enough to see a gap in the provision of a much required service. They were also clever enough to ensure they did not infringe Scottish law when providing their service. To avoid criminal prosecution, 'parsons' would sign a wedding certificate merely certifying that they had witnessed a particular couple exchange the binding promises of marriage. Nothing more was required for a Scottish marriage to be legal.

For their pains the 'parsons' were paid anything from three or four shillings to as many pounds.

It was the bridegroom more so than the 'parson' who was in danger of prosecution following the mad dash to Scotland. Any bridegroom who ran away with an heiress, whether he later married her or not, could be convicted of kidnapping. But again there was a loophole in the law. To protect the groom, all the heiress had to do was ensure it was she rather than he who played the role of the abductor, carrying off her lover, who could then be accused of no greater crime than weakness of character.

"*Those whom God has joined together, Let no man put asunder.*"

159

ROYALTY

ome royal weddings have had more influence on world history than major battles. Power has been gained, wars started, trade routes developed and empires created all because of well planned marital alliances.

The Christian religions owe a lot to one particular wedding. Back in the fifth century, the marriage of one Lady Bertha to the kind Ethelbert of Kent prepared the way for the conversion of England to Christianity.

Bertha was the daughter of Charibert of Frankfurt. And, like most other Germans at the time, she practised the Christian faith. However, her chosen husband did not. Many years before the marriage, Christian crusaders had been driven out of England by the Saxons. The English were all pagans, Charibert agreed to his daughter marrying Ethelbert only if she was permitted to profess her own religion. The result was that Bertha's chaplain was admitted to the English court and a ruined church was again allocated for Christian worship. From these two seeds the faith spread to become dominant for many centuries.

ETHELRED AND EMMA

The descendants of Bertha and Ethelbert continued to shape English history through marriage.

When Ethelred the Unready (we are not exactly sure why he was called that) married Emma of Normandy in the year 1002, he unwittingly laid the foundations for the Norman Invasion, an event destined to become one of the most significant in English history.

Ethelred and Emma had a son who became known as Edward the Confessor after he claimed the Throne of England in 1046.

Because his father had died when he was a child and his mother remarried, Edward was raised by relatives in Normandy, France, rather than in England. So, as king, he naturally leaned towards his Norman kinsfolk and conferred the highest offices, in both Church and State, upon Norman courtiers and ecclesiastics. Edward also chose a Frenchman–the Duke of Normandy–for his heir. This Duke was later to be known in England as William the Conqueror.

After Edward's death, the English people did not accept his choice of heir. When William came to claim the Throne he was opposed by the people's choice, a Saxon, Harold II. The two

contenders fought over the title in the famous Battle of Hastings. William won, became king in 1066 and today the British are descendant from this Norman line.

It was not until William's youngest son, Henry I, married Matilda of Scotland that the old Saxon blood was brought back to the English royal house. Once this marriage took place, both the Normans and the Saxons were appeased and England became a strong and stable country.

A HAPPY ENDING TO THE WARS OF THE ROSES

It was also a marriage which really put an end to the Wars of the Roses. Henry VII reunited the House of Lancaster with the House of York and finally settled the thirty year dispute over which branch of the royal family was rightfully entitled to the Crown by choosing Elizabeth of York as his bride. From this marriage began the great Tudor dynasty.

HENRY VIII AND ANNE BOLEYN

One of the last marriages to substantially change the direction of history was the marriage of Henry VIII to Anne Boleyn. Just as Rome first began her ascendancy in England through the marriage of Bertha and Ethelbert, so her descent was made complete following the second marriage of that country's most headstrong king.

By 1533, the Church of Rome was in decline and the Reformation movement had began to spread over Germany and Scotland. But it had not yet reached England. It was not until Henry cast his longing eyes upon Anne Boleyn, only to find he could not acquire a release from his existing marriage to Catherine of Aragon, that he and his court began to look seriously at an alternative religious practice.

After many quarrels with Pope Clement VII, Henry denied the Pope had authority over England and secretly married Anne Boleyn. The Archbishop of Canterbury Thomas Cranmer, acting without authority on the Pope's behalf, declared the marriage of Henry and Catherine null and void. Anne was then crowned queen. Poor Catherine was condemned to life in the Tower of London.

The Act of Supremacy, passed by Parliament in 1538 at Henry's insistence, made the Church of England a separate institution from the Church of Rome and firmly established the Reformation in yet another empire.

TODAY'S ERA OF ROMANCE

Modern royal weddings have been a little less influential than those in the past, but what they have lost in strategy they make up for in romance.

Queen Victoria's marriage to Albert Saxe-Coburg-Gotha, on 10 February 1840, followed from a courtship which began in childhood. The couple were very much in love.

As guests looked down the aisle of the chapel in St. James Palace on that day they saw a tiny bride dressed in white satin trimmed with a very deep flounce of old Honiton lace. She was

followed by twelve train-bearers also dressed in white satin and each carrying a bouquet of white roses. The train-bearers were necessary to manoeuvre the heavy eighteen foot-long train as the bride walked to the altar.

Exquisite jewellery, including a Turkish diamond necklace with matching earrings and a sapphire brooch given to the bride by Albert as a wedding present, compensated for the plainness of Victorian dress and highlighted the bride's liking for large gem stones.

England's longest serving monarch later described her wedding day as the most memorable day in her life. So that she could enjoy it fully she had lifted her tulle veil back off her face during the ceremony and, unwittingly, by this slight action she put an end to a very old wedding tradition.

Victoria and Albert's wedding cake stood out as strikingly for guests at the wedding feast as the Victorian era does in history today. The cake cut by the royal couple weighed three hundred pounds (136.14 kilograms) and was crowned with an ice sculpture of Britannia–the female personification of Britain in the form of a woman wearing a helmet and holding a shield and trident as if ready for battle. The ice sculpture was surrounded by sugar cupids.

——— DUKE AND DUCHESS BECAME KING AND QUEEN ———

When Lady Elizabeth Bowes-Lyon (now Queen Elizabeth the Queen Mother) married the Duke of York on 26 April 1923, she had no idea she was destined to become the next queen of England. So, by royal standards this marriage was a quiet affair. Prior to the wedding the young Duchess was totally unknown to the world. Both she and the Duke of York had always shied away from publicity as much as possible.

Lady Elizabeth chose a typical 1920s design for her wedding dress. It was made in ivory chiffon moire, cut in a slender medieval style, with a square neckline and dropped waistline. It was trimmed with silver lame. The wedding was held in Westminster Abbey and received little publicity except for a report in the London papers and women's fashion magazines.

——— A CAKE MADE UP FROM THE WAR ALLOWANCE ———

In contrast to the wedding of her parents, Princess Elizabeth Windsor's marriage to Lieutenant Philip Mountbatten on 29 November 1947 was celebrated throughout the British Commonwealth. The War was over and this was the first occasion Britain had had to celebrate since Germany's defeat.

The wedding was also popular because, after the harsh years of war, it brought romance back into style. It was a fairy-tale wedding. Not only was a beautiful princess involved, but the handsome prince had turned down his own rights to the Crown of the Royal House of Greece, choosing instead England and Elizabeth.

England had not yet regained its footing following the War. The country was in the grips of an economic crisis. So Princess Elizabeth's wedding was, by necessity, a relatively scant affair. At the time, food rations were scarcer than they had been during the war years and, just like

everyone else in England, the royal family was subject to government restrictions. Food, drink and even clothing for the wedding and the bride's trousseau had to be obtained on war coupons, from donations, or from whatever could be found in the royal cellars.

During her four month engagement, Princess Elizabeth received presents from across the Commonwealth. Many families who considered it a matter of national prestige that the heir to their Throne should look right donated clothing coupons from their meagre allowance of eighteen per year for each adult, but the Princess would include very few new dresses in her trousseau.

The design of the twenty-one year old bride's wedding-dress was based on delicate Botticelli curves. Scattered over the ivory satin bodice and gown were garlands of white York roses (signifying the House of York) framed with raised pearls. Each rose was entwined with an ear of corn minutely embroidered with crystal. Star flowers and orange blossoms also featured on reverse embroidered tulle on satin and satin on tulle–the whole encrusted with more pearls and crystal.

A simple two-strand string of pearls was all the Princess wore to adorn the dress. They were a gift from the King and she was never without them.

Princess Elizabeth's wedding cake was made in Edinburgh by the firm McVittie and Price, the same firm which had made the cake for her parents' wedding twenty-four years earlier. The design of the five hundred pound (226.80 kilograms) cake was Grecian and it stood nine feet high (just under three metres). More than one thousand people could have received a slice if it had been consumed in its entirety on the wedding day.

The main feature of the four-tiered cake was a silver quaigh, a type of drinking-cup, which had been bought in Edinburgh through the Antiquarian Society as a gift for the royal couple. The quaigh was filled with fresh flowers and streamers of flowers and leaves fell from its handles to rest on the solid silver cake base. Each of the four tiers were separated by matching antique silver pillars, which had also supported many earlier royal wedding cakes.

Overall the cake was elaborately decorated. The bottom tier featured Princess Elizabeth's coat-of-arms in the centre and had a scene of Balmoral Castle on the left-hand side, with a corresponding scene of Windsor Castle on the right. The second tier showed the coat-of-arms of Lieutenant Mountbatten, with his interests and sports surrounding it. The third-tier had the badge of the Grenadier Guards in the centre, with Princess Elizabeth's interests on either side. On the top tier the centrepiece was the badge of the Sea Rangers, topped off with a large EW and PM, the initials of the bride and groom. Between each of these emblems and all around the cake sugar cupids appeared in various attitudes. Altogether many hundreds of pieces of sugar-work were made individually and fitted onto the cake to produce the overall effect.

The end result was a far cry from the cake decorated with cardboard many women's magazines predicted the Princess would be forced to accept because of the severe shortage of sugar.

The ingredients for the wedding cake were, wherever possible, drawn from Empire sources. India and Australia donated spices and dried fruit for the wedding cake. Small envelopes of sugar were sent in from across the country so that the cake could be iced. It seemed everyone who could, contributed something. Australia's contribution of bundles of dried fruits, were collected by the Girl Guides and especially shipped to England in time for inclusion. Each tier of the cake was baked for eight to ten hours in the oven.

ROYALTY ARE A SUPERSTITIOUS LOT

Princess Margaret, the future Queen's sister, told friends that Princess Elizabeth showed quite a superstitious nature in the months leading up to her wedding and insisted upon having all the traditional trappings for a bride's good fortune, including something old, something new, something borrowed and something blue.

The something old was a pair of sandal-like shoes which the Princess had worn many times before and found very comfortable. For something borrowed she wore a diamond tiara, which belonged to the Queen Mother. There was a blue lovers' knot stitched into the lining of the wedding dress. And the something new, of course, was the wedding dress itself, which had not been finished until the very last minute–another old superstition observed.

Although urged by her sister, Princess Elizabeth refused to put on her wedding dress the night before the wedding in case it brought ill luck. On the day of her wedding she refused to look into the mirror to dress. Instead she allowed herself to be guided completely by the opinions of her bridesmaids.

A CAKE TO MAKE DREAMS COME TRUE

According to a report in *The Australian Woman's Weekly* before the royal wedding, Princess Elizabeth was not the only superstitious young lady in England in 1947. *The Weekly* predicted that on the night of the wedding: "Hundreds of young girls throughout the Empire will sleep on a piece of the Princess's wedding cake in the hope of dreaming of their own true love."

These ladies were able to obtain a piece of the wedding cake because there were actually ten official cakes made for the occasion. Each was donated by cake firms and all bar the one described earlier were given to various organisations and clubs throughout the British Empire to be cut and distributed.

About the only hitch at Princess Elizabeth and Philip's wedding was their first attempt to cut their wedding cake. Philip was wearing his naval uniform and carried his grandfather's (Prince Louis of Battenburg) sword for the occasion. The sword was a well used and much loved relic of old battles. When the time came for the bride and groom to cut the cake, in traditional naval style with the bridegroom's sword, the old weapon was so blunt it would not even pierce the marzipan icing.

When the first wedge of cake was finally removed it contained many tiny surprises for each of

the bridesmaids. A token thimble, gold threepence, lucky donkey, wedding ring, bachelor's button, horseshoe and dove had all been hidden within this one slice.

PRINCESS MARGARET, AND HER CHAMPION

Princess Margaret went to the top chef in England when it came time for the baking of her wedding cake. Morecombe pastry chef David Ronald Adams had already won one thousand awards for cake decorating by the time he received the royal order for the wedding held on 6 May 1960. The fact that this cake was for a Princess did little to faze the accomplished chef, he proudly wore his own title–Champion Confectioner of England and Wales.

WHEN A COMMONER WEDS A KING

Lady Diana Spencer, the Princess of Wales, was most notable at her wedding to Prince Charles on 29 July 1981 because she was the first commoner to marry an heir to the British Throne for more than three hundred years. This did not stop her from putting on an elaborate show. The estimated overall cost of this royal wedding was more than half a million pounds. Half of this sum was spent on security alone.

The cost of Lady Diana's wedding dress, veil, train and shoes was about twenty five thousand pounds. The wedding dress was made of ivory pure silk taffeta with embroidered lace panels at the back and front of the bodice. Both the dress and the tulle veil were hand embroidered with mother-of-pearl sequins and real pearls, as were her matching silk slippers. But the highlight of the dress was the sweeping twenty-five foot train trimmed with lace.

The bride carried a bouquet made up of gardenias, golden roses, orchids, stephanotis, lilies of the valley, fresias, myrtle and veronica.

At the reception in Buckingham Palace, Prince Charles and Lady Diana cut a hexagonal wedding cake which stood five foot high (1.5 metres) and weighed two hundred and twenty five pounds (101.65 kilograms). The cake was made and decorated by the Royal Navy's Cooking School, HMS 'Penbroke'. Chief Petty Officer David Avery (nicknamed Able Cakeman Avery) was in charge of the baking and decorating operation.

When told he had the honour of making the royal wedding cake, Chef Avery declared he would bake the biggest, richest cake ever to have come out of the Naval Cookery School. He did, but no one knows how. The recipe, which he did not write down, has never been revealed.

However, we do know cake preparations for the July wedding commenced in early April. It took two full days just to sort the fruit to be included. The total cooking time was one afternoon and a full night and the largest tier was in the oven for eight hours.

Chef Avery designed the cake decoration himself, but had to obtain Palace approval. It was Lady Diana who gave the royal okay, after she had seen illustrations of each of the tiers.

It was not the baking or decorating of the cake which gave the chef the greatest worry. Rather, it

was the problem of transporting a five-foot high, fragile masterpiece on a three-hour trip from the Naval School's kitchen to Buckingham Palace.

In the end the cake travelled well and was given pride of place at the three course wedding breakfast, which was attended by one hundred and eighteen of the royal couple's closest friends and relatives. At the end of the breakfast the Prince and Princess cut the cake using Prince Charles' ceremonial sword.

DEFENCE FORCE CHEFS MAKE GOOD COOKS

Like Prince Charles, Prince Andrew asked the arm of the Royal Defence Forces under which he served to bake and decorate his wedding cake. Prince Andrew and Sarah Ferguson cut a cake prepared by the Royal Navy's supply school at HMS Raleigh in Cornwall.

NO FUSSY RETINUE FOR PRINCESS ANNE

Colour television was in fashion by the time Princess Anne married Captain Mark Phillips on 14 November 1973 and five hundred million people are estimated to have enjoyed the entertainment.

But still, in comparison to most royal weddings, this was a quiet family affair. Prior to her marriage Princess Anne had been a bridesmaid five times. When her own turn came to be honoured as the bride she declared she had had enough of all the fussy retinue of child attendants and other ceremony. The Princess decided for her wedding she was going to dispose of as many traditional royal customs as she could. Only Lady Sarah Armstrong-Jones and Prince Edward attended the bride. There was no mention of anything borrowed, or of anything blue. And, unlike her mother's, Princess Anne's shoes certainly did not constitute something old. Her shoes were especially made from white satin and lined with gold.

Even Princess Anne's wedding cake defied tradition. The cake was made and decorated by the Army Catering Corps and from the outside looked just like a wedding cake should. But, contrary to normal practice, underneath the royal icing the cake had only a token smudge of marzipan, because Princess Anne does not enjoy the taste.

At the end of this wedding, the royal family, including the Queen and Prince Charles, who happened to also be celebrating his birthday, went back to the palace and watched the event all over again on television.